Syntactic Change and Syntactic Reconstruction: A Tagmemic Approach

SUMMER INSTITUTE OF LINGUISTICS

PUBLICATIONS IN LINGUISTICS

Publication Number 68

EDITORS

Desmond C. Derbyshire
*Summer Institute
of Linguistics*

Virgil L. Poulter
*University of Texas
at Arlington*

ASSISTANT EDITORS

Alan C. Wares   Iris M. Wares

CONSULTING EDITORS

Doris A. Bartholomew
Pamela M. Bendor-Samuel
Robert Dooley
Austin Hale
Phyllis Healey

Robert E. Longacre
Eugene E. Loos
William R. Merrifield
Kenneth L. Pike
Viola G. Waterhouse

Syntactic Change and Syntactic Reconstruction: A Tagmemic Approach

John R. Costello

A PUBLICATION OF
    THE SUMMER INSTITUTE OF LINGUISTICS
    and
    THE UNIVERSITY OF TEXAS AT ARLINGTON

1983

ISBN 0-88312-092-5

Library of Congress Catalog Card No.: 83-60279

© 1983 by the Summer Institute of Linguistics, Inc.

All rights reserved.

Copies of this publication and other publications of the Summer Institute of Linguistics may be obtained from

>Bookstore
>Summer Institute of Linguistics
>7500 W. Camp Wisdom Rd.
>Dallas, TX   75236

To Elizabeth and Daniel

"Language reflects the image of God, so could you expect it to be anything other than beautiful, elegantly patterned, glorious, and difficult?"

Kenneth L. Pike

Contents

Preface xi
Acknowledgments xxi
Abbreviations and Symbols xxiii
Introduction xxvii

1. The Tagmeme, the Syntagmeme, and Comparative Reconstruction
   1.1. The Tagmeme 1
   1.2. The Syntagmeme 5
   1.3. Excursus: Horizontal and Vertical Etic Units 7
   1.4. Comparative Reconstruction 9

2. Tagmemic and Syntagmemic Change
   2.1. One-to-one Replacement 12
   2.2. Merger 20
   2.3. Split 28
   2.4. Amorphous Loss or Disappearance 36
   2.5. Amorphous Gain or Increment 37

3. Tagmemic, Syntagmemic, Allotagmatic, and Allosyntagmatic Reconstruction
   3.1. One-to-one Replacement 39
   3.2. Merger 46
   3.3. Split 51
   3.4. Amorphous Loss or Disappearance 66
   3.5. Amorphous Gain or Increment 67

4. Syntactosemantic Reconstruction
   4.1. Tagmemic 68
   4.2. Syntagmemic 69

Bibliography 71
Index 77

List of Figures

Figure 1	3
Figure 2	4
Figure 3	6
Figure 4	7
Figure 5	10
Figure 6	13
Figure 7	14
Figure 8	15
Figure 9	16
Figure 10	19
Figure 11	21
Figure 12	22
Figure 13	23
Figure 14	25
Figure 15	26
Figure 16	26
Figure 17	29
Figure 18	30
Figure 19	32
Figure 20	33
Figure 21	34
Figure 22	35
Figure 23	35
Figure 24	37
Figure 25	38
Figure 26	40
Figure 27	41
Figure 28	42
Figure 29	43
Figure 30	45
Figure 31	47
Figure 32	47

Contents

Figure 33 48
Figure 34 49
Figure 35 58
Figure 36 58
Figure 37 59
Figure 38 60
Figure 39 61
Figure 40 62
Figure 41 62
Figure 42 63
Figure 43 64

Preface

The purpose of this book is to demonstrate that it is possible to reconstruct syntactic constructions, their constituents, and the functions of these constituents for a protolanguage by applying certain procedures of internal and comparative reconstruction to data from the daughter languages concerned. A natural question to ask is, "Why would one want to reconstruct the syntactic constructions, their constituents, and the functions of these constituents for a protolanguage?" As far as this writer is concerned, the answer to that question follows from the opening statement of part 2 of *The Port-Royal Grammar* (Arnold and Lancelot 1660), entitled "The principles and reasons on which the various forms of the signification of words are founded":

> Until now we have only considered the material element of speech, and that which is common, at least as far as sound is concerned, to both man and parrots.
> It remains for us to examine the spiritual element of speech which constitutes one of the greatest advantages which man has over all the other animals, and which is one of the proofs of man's reason. This is the use which we make of it for signifying our thoughts. . . .

To be sure, the more we investigate this "spiritual element of speech," the more we will learn about "man's reason." Certainly one of the aspects of language that deserves investigation is that of change, since change in language indicates a change in "signifying our thoughts."

There is still much to be learned about language change, but unfortunately one of the problems involved in investigating change in most of the world's languages is the absence of sufficient recorded material from older periods to enable us to observe and interpret the bulk of the changes. This deficiency may be overcome by reconstructing earlier stages of a language now unavailable to us; it is toward this end that the present work was conceived.

The model of grammar followed here is that of tagmemics as

presented in Pike and Pike (1982) (with some minor modifications). In this framework, the constituents of syntactic constructions are called tagmemes, and the syntactic constructions themselves are referred to as syntagmemes. In Pike and Pike (1982), unlike many earlier works on tagmemics (e.g., Longacre 1964, Brend 1968, and Cook 1969), the tagmeme is presented as having four cells rather than two: "The tagmeme is a constituent of a construction [i.e., a syntagmeme—JC] seen from the point of view of its four general features [i.e., cells—JC]: *slot, class, role,* and *cohesion.* . . . Each feature is closely related to each of the other three. . . . In *Bill hit Joe, Bill*—which is a member of the class Proper Noun Root—fills the slot of *subject* which has the role *actor.* . . . [An] English example of cohesion is the number of the subject which governs the number in the verb *(He sells cars* versus *They sell cars)*" (p. 33). The major concern in discussing the reconstruction of tagmemes in the present work will be the (syntactic) *slot* and the (manifesting) *class.* (Syntactosemantic) *role* and its reconstruction will be discussed in 2.2.1.1 in examples dealing with levels of grammar above the sentence, and also in chapter 4. As a rule, *cohesion* will not be dealt with explicitly.

As Longacre (1964) states, the concepts of the syntagmeme and the tagmeme are correlative: "Syntagmemes cannot exist without component elements, i.e., tagmemes. On the other hand, tagmemes exist only by virtue of placement in one or more syntagmemes" (p. 15). Moreover, "Typically, syntagmemes of one structural level manifest tagmemes of the next highest level" (p. 17).

Tagmemics is squarely based on the structuralist notions of etic and emic units. Following Cook (1969:19), we may say that

Syntagmas (and allosyntagmas) are to syntagmemes, what
Tagmas (and allotagmas) are to tagmemes, what
Morphs (and allomorphs) are to morphemes, and what
Phones (and allophones) are to phonemes.

Thus it is only natural that the framework for reconstruction that has been chosen for the present work is the structuralist one, which makes extensive use of the contrastive and characteristic environments of linguistic units (cf. Hoenigswald 1960).

Some readers who are interested in generative grammar (which shows little interest in "surface structure" phenomena) may be inclined to eschew an application of structuralist procedures of reconstruction to syntactic data viewed in an essentially structuralist framework. In response to this, it is important to point out that whenever one is reconstructing from a later to an earlier stage of a language, the input data that one must begin with are surface structure phenomena of the later stage, and the reconstructions that one achieves are surface structure phenomena of an earlier stage. That this applies ultimately to generativist as well as to structuralist diachronic work in reconstruction may be seen upon considering the following steps (often taken for granted) leading, for example, to a comparative phonological reconstruction.

First, one must determine that the languages from which one is taking data are genealogically related (cf. Greenberg 1957:35–45). Secondly, one must determine the subgroupings within the family of languages under consideration (cf. Greenberg 1957:46–56). Thirdly, one must select as a data base bona fide sound-meaning correspondences (etymologies) shared by the daughter languages under consideration (cf. Greenberg 1957:45). Fourthly, one must subject these etymologies to structuralist procedures of morphological and phonological internal reconstruction (cf. Hoenigswald 1960:68f., 98ff., 151, 158; Marchand 1956; and Chafe 1959). Fifthly, one must extract from the data base that results from internal reconstruction sets of phonological correspondences shared by the daughter languages. Sixthly, employing the correspondence sets of the daughter languages, one may, by applying structuralist procedures, reconstruct protophonemes of the parent language (cf. Hoenigswald 1960:119–43). So far, then, the only procedures that have been employed are structuralist ones. As may be seen in generative discussions found in works like King (1969), Kiparsky (1971), and Lehmann (1973), no generative diachronic treatments of such topics as Grimm's Law, Verner's Law, and Grassmann's Law (to mention just a few), would have been possible unless these six steps had already been carried out. In other words, generative diachronic phonology involving reconstructed data is dependent upon the application of structuralist procedures of reconstruction to surface structure linguistic units from daughter languages in order to achieve surface structure linguistic units in protolanguages. The same holds true, mutatis mutandis, for studies in diachronic morphology and diachronic syntax.

In the present work, it is demonstrated that the procedures of comparative morphological (and phonological) reconstruction as presented in Hoenigswald (1960) may be applied in comparative tagmemic and comparative syntagmemic reconstruction essentially because tagmemes and syntagmemes are subject to the same types of replacement patterns as morphemes (and in parallel fashion, phonemes), namely, one-to-one replacement, merger, split (including the subtypes common to all: regular replacement, replacement by "semantic change," replacement by innovation, and replacement by borrowing), amorphous loss, and amorphous gain. Just as Hoenigswald (1960:70, 134ff.) emphasizes that in comparative morphemic and comparative phonemic reconstruction the primary goal is the protomorpheme and the protophoneme, respectively, so it is stressed here (cf. chapter 3) that the primary goal of comparative tagmemic and comparative syntagmemic reconstruction is the prototagmeme and the protosyntagmeme (although a principle is proposed in chapter 1 whereby, under certain conditions, protoallotagmas and protoallosyntagmas may be inferred). In other words, emic, not etic, units are the primary concern of all comparative reconstruction. Unfortunately some linguists who overlook this point in the existing literature come to realize it for themselves only after reflecting on reconstruction in general, and then, (erroneously) assuming that comparative reconstruction claims consistently to be able to retrieve etic units that manifest emic units, see in this limitation a failure of the comparative method. Moreover, just as Hoenigswald (1960:70 et passim) points out that a major achievement of comparative morphemic and comparative phonemic reconstruction is to reverse mergers (and, as a byproduct of this, retrieve earlier contrasts, i.e., protoemic units), but that such phenomena as advanced analogical change and duplicate merger (cf. Hoenigswald 1960:32, 110, 125, 132) may not be retrievable, depending upon the number of daughter languages available to the investigator, so the same merits and limits are pointed out below, mutatis mutandis, for comparative tagmemic and comparative syntagmemic reconstruction.

From my own work in generative grammar (cf. Costello 1977, 1978b, and 1980) I am aware that a nontagmemic approach to syntax might well preclude viewing syntactic data as I do here. Surveying the situation from a generative point of view, Lightfoot (1979:155) refers to ". . . the self-evident lack of parallelism [of syntactic reconstruction] with phonological work. . . ." Cf. also Lightfoot (1980), passim.

Moreover, associating comparative reconstruction too closely with comparative phonemic reconstruction to the neglect of comparative morphemic reconstruction may also preclude an application of the procedures of comparative reconstruction to syntax. Later on in his book, Lightfoot states that "there is no analogous basis [i.e., analogous to phonology—JC] in syntax for the comparative method; there is no finite set of sentences occurring in parallel positions across languages in a finite set of cognate (presumably discourse) contexts" (p. 163). True, the set of sentences (and the set of syntagmemes) in a language is, unlike the set of phonemes, not finite; however, the parallels are not to be sought between comparative syntagmemic reconstruction and comparative phonemic reconstruction, but rather between comparative syntagmemic reconstruction and comparative morphemic reconstruction. The set of syntagmemes in a language, like the set of morphemes, is potentially infinite; moreover, syntagmemes, like morphemes, have contrastive and characteristic environments, various etic manifestations, and correspondences (with subtypes) in sister languages—in other words, all of the qualities that are necessary for comparative reconstruction, as will be shown.

Recently a great deal has been written about the difference between "descriptive" and "explanatory" approaches to syntax. For example, with respect to diachronic syntax in particular, Lehmann (1974:6) writes, "An explanatory syntax is now possible because of two recent developments in linguistics: the study of syntax for its underlying patterns, which owes much of its impetus to the work of Noam Chomsky (1965), and the typological framework for syntax which is based in great part on an important essay of Joseph Greenberg (1966)." As examples of a descriptive syntax, Lehmann (1974:3f.) cites the collections of data in works such as Schwyzer's (1939–53) *Griechische Grammatik,* Miklosich's (1868–74) *Vergleichende Grammatik der slavischen Sprachen,* and Grimm's (1870–98) *Deutsche Grammatik.* As an example of an explanation of a syntactic pattern (albeit a sporadic phenomenon), Lehmann cites Wackernagel's discussion of case assimilation or attraction in Ancient Greek. Since one must have data before one can explain them, one's primary concern with respect to a protolanguage is to reconstruct the data, and one's secondary concern—quite apart from reconstruction—is to explain them (cf. also Lightfoot 1979:158f.) Certainly Hoenigswald and others have demonstrated that the reconstruction of the phonology and morphology of a protolanguage can be accomplished independently of an explanation of the reconstructed data that relies on structuralist (or any other) principles. Proceeding from this point, one might ask if our secondary concern, an explanatory syntax of the protolanguage (and daughter languages), would be precluded because the data were reconstructed within the theoretical framework of tagmemics, rather than the theoretical frameworks mentioned by Lehmann? Definitely not. It is important to distinguish between a problem in syntax and a problem pertaining to a particular syntactic framework. A problem in syntax (like case assimilation) is independent of a model of grammar. Sooner or later an explanation of a problem in syntax will be realized, provided that one sees explaining, rather than collecting and describing data, as his task; the value of the explanation is, however, always internal to the theoretical framework in which it is formulated. As Longacre (1964:15, footnote 10) observes, "It is essential that a theory and its applications be judged against the background of its own basic assumptions, not against the background of alien assumptions." Wackernagel's formulation and explanation of the syntactic problem of case assimilation must needs differ from those of a tagmemicist or a generativist, but the fact remains that the problem may be formulated and explained in each of the three frameworks.

The directions for syntactic reconstruction in recent years were set with the publication of Lehmann's *Proto-Indo-European Syntax* in 1974. As the title of his book indicates, Lehmann's main concern is the syntax of Proto-Indo-European; however, the volume also contains discussion of syntactic reconstruction as a topic in itself. The particular aspect of syntactic reconstruction that is developed is the reconstruction of word order typology (cf. Greenberg 1966), which Lehmann refers to as "the reconstruction of syntactic patterns" (p. 5).

The model of grammar employed by Lehmann is essentially that of case grammar (cf. Fillmore 1968). That is, "the grammar proposed . . . generates nouns through abstract syntactosemantic categories which have been called cases but which [Lehmann refers] to as K, from Panini's term *kāraka* for underlying case categories" (p. 10). In keeping with this, Lehmann proposes a number of phrase structure rules which he assumes are universal (p. 10), and, in order to modify the sequence of elements in the terminal string produced by the phrase structure rules, a "principle . . . which produces the fundamental order in the sentences of each language." The formulation of this is as follows:

$$\# \, Q \, V \, (N^{Obj.}) \, (N^{Mod.}) \, \# \longrightarrow \left\{ \begin{array}{l} \# \, Q \, V \, (N^{Obj.}) \, (N^{Mod.}) \, \# \\ \# \, (N^{Mod.}) \, (N^{Obj.}) \, V \, Q \, \# \end{array} \right\}$$

"By this principle, noun objects ($N^{Obj.}$) are placed either before or after verbs. If objects are placed before verbs, the verb is followed by the categorial markers for qualifiers. If objects are placed after verbs, the Q categorial markers precede the verbs. Further, nominal modifiers ($N^{Mod.}$) are placed on the opposite side of nouns from that on which verbs stand with regard to their objects. This principle brings about the distinguishing characteristics of verb-object (VO) and object-verb (OV) languages" (p. 12). Lehmann also mentions transformational rules which ". . . are included for the following processes: Topicalization, Complementation, Deletion, as of equivalent noun phrases, Agreement [formulation on pp. 72f. in his book], Relativization and relative clause reduction [formulated on p. 58 of his book] [and] Transportation of elements, such as the negative qualifier. In addition there are numerous rules which bring about the correct sequences and patterns in the surface structure; these are often referred to as 'housekeeping rules'" (p. 13). Clearly, then, Lehmann's claim that Proto-Indo-European was OV is one that refers to this syntactic surface structure, not to its underlying structures. It is important to bear this in mind, especially since other linguists who have been following Lehmann's approach to diachronic syntax have evidently been less specific in their claims. Consider, for example, the following statement by Lightfoot (1979:155): "In recent years there has been a great deal of work on syntactic reconstruction; witness Friedrich (1975), Jacobs (1975), Lehmann (1974), and several of the papers in Li (1975b and 1977) and the references cited there. . . . In many cases it is even unclear what the authors claim to be reconstructing, whether sentences or (fragments of) grammars of the protolanguage. For example, the claim that Proto-Indo-European was SOV might be a claim about the underlying order of initial structures or a claim about statistical probabilities of surface structures of sentences."

As a framework for reconstruction, Lehmann has chosen to employ the implicational universals which Greenberg (1966) derived from his typological studies. Essentially, Lehmann reconstructs the basic word order pattern of a Proto-Indo-European construction by determining the pattern of this construction in a consistently VO language and in a consistently OV language, and then comparing the consistent patterns of this construction with the patterns of the corresponding construction in what are considered to be the archaic daughter languages of Proto-Indo-European. (The technique itself was anticipated some years earlier than the publication of Lehmann's book, as the following quotation from Jakobson's article, "Typological Studies and Their Contribution to Historical and Comparative Linguistics" (1962:530) shows: "What can typological studies contribute to historical comparative linguistics? In Greenberg's view, the typology of languages adds to 'our predictive power since from a given synchronic system certain developments will be highly likely, others have less probability, and still others may be practically excluded'.... Schlegel, the anticipator of comparative linguistics and typology, described the historian as a prophet predicting backward. Our 'predictive power' in reconstruction gains support from typological studies.") By way of illustration, Lehmann (1974:15) notes that the pattern of the simple predicate is consistently VO in Arabic, and consistently OV in Turkish. He then observes that there is verb-final word order in Hittite (p. 34), early Greek, early Latin (p. 35), and Vedic Sanskrit (passim), and concludes that "... on the basis of patterns such as those cited from the early dialects, Proto-Indo-European can be assumed to be OV" (p. 39). To be sure, this simplified and condensed version of Lehmann's methodology obscures the (often staggering) complexity encountered in this approach to reconstruction, as is indicated among the final qualifying remarks of *Proto-Indo-European Syntax:* "Proto-Indo-European itself must have been subjected to various influences. As a result its stages cannot be sketched with certainty. The common trend towards VO patterning, apparent even in Anatolian, indicates however that late Proto-Indo-European must have been changing from an OV structure. To what extent its earlier structure was consistently OV cannot be ascertained, at least for the present" (p. 250). Thus, what Lehmann has attempted to do is reconstruct the word order typology of Proto-Indo-European.

In reviewing the following criticisms that have been expressed concerning the typological reconstruction of word order patterns, with particular reference to Lehmann's *Proto-Indo-European Syntax*, I will briefly explain how comparative tagmemic and comparative syntagmemic reconstruction bypass these objections; a more thorough discussion of the work of Lehmann (and others) in connection with this method, and the comments that have been published concerning it, though desirable, would go beyond the scope of the present work. In his monograph entitled *Linguistic Reconstruction: Its Potentials and Limitations in New Perspective,* H. Birnbaum (1977) expresses two interesting reservations with respect to Lehmann's work. In the first, Birnbaum notes "the purely hypothetical, and thus questionable, nature of the underlying syntactic patterns (deep structures) posited by Lehmann, which are not susceptible to empirical corroboration" (p. 38). As far as this point is concerned, it must be noted that it is not only Lehmann's (case grammar) underlying syntactic patterns or deep structures that are not susceptible to empirical corroboration; the same could be said of the deep structures not only of other linguists working within the framework of case grammar, e.g., Fillmore (1968) and Traugott (1972), but also of linguists working within other generative frameworks. As Lyons (1970:41) states, for example: "Linguistic theory should be concerned, then, with the justification of grammars. Chomsky goes on to consider the possibility of formulating criteria for deciding whether a particular grammar is the best one possible for the data. He concludes that even this goal—the formulation of a *decision procedure*—is too ambitious. The most that can be expected is that linguistic theory should provide criteria (an evaluation procedure) for choosing between alternative grammars. *In other words, we cannot hope to say whether a particular description of the data is correct, in any absolute sense, but only that it is more correct than some alternative description of the same data* [italics mine—JC]." Birnbaum's first criticism could hardly be applied to the tagmemic model that has been chosen for the present work, for the very notions of deep and surface structure as they are used in generative literature are not applicable in an approach where, at all grammatical levels, the designation of underlying function[1] (at times inadequately indicated in the deep structure of generative grammars) is always inextricably correlated with its manifestation.

Moreover, in view of the approach to transformations that is followed here, this exemption from Birnbaum's criticism holds true for the "input" as well as the "output" structures linked by these operations.

As Longacre states, "A further concept of tagmemics is the matrix

---

1. It is worthy of note that Jesperson's approach to "underlying notions" in his *Analytic Syntax* and elsewhere closely resembles the one taken by Pike in his development of tagmemic theory (cf. Jespersen 1937:vi, 22, 24, et passim).

whose model is space in n dimensions (one-dimensional matrices are trivial unless in a system of matrices with further dimensions). In grammar this develops the notion of relatedness in logical space by arranging syntagmemes or tagmemes in a system of coordinates. Like items are made contiguous; unlike items separated. Transformation relations take their place among parameters which relate constructions." (Cf. also Longacre 1964:16, Longacre 1965:72, Heller and Macris 1979:209, and Bowers 1981: 15–50, particularly p. 46.)

Birnbaum's (1977:38) second criticism of Lehmann's approach has to do with the "exaggerated significance attributed by [Lehmann] to the sequential arrangement of surface structures (notably, the distinction of OV vs. VO structures) for a language or, in any case, a certain evolutionary phase of a language which, typologically, by all we can surmise about it was highly flexible as to work order" (p. 38). However, in my opinion, there is an important aspect of the problems of word order typology, the universals derived therefrom, and their application in typological reconstruction which must be mentioned even before considering Birnbaum's remarks, namely that, with all due respect to Greenberg's work, it is not certain that the correlates that emerged from the patterns in the relatively small number of "consistent" languages that he investigated will hold once the remainder of the world's few thousand languages are investigated. For, as Greenberg himself stated in the opening sentence of his 1966 article, "Some Universals of Grammar with Particular Reference to the Order of Meaningful Elements," "The tentative nature of the conclusions set forth here should be evident to the reader" (p. 73). In this respect as well as in others, then, Lehmann's (1974:251) final qualifying remarks concerning the preliminary nature of his treatment of Proto-Indo-European syntax are well founded.

Returning now to Birnbaum's second criticism, it should be noted that although his objection is valid in the strictest sense, the following points concerning Lehmann's claims must be taken into consideration: (a) Lehmann (p. 250) states that late Proto-Indo-European must have been changing from an OV structure, and more importantly, that at least for the present it cannot be ascertained to what extent the earlier structure of Proto-Indo-European was consistently OV; and (b) Lehmann qualifies his statements concerning word order patterns in Proto-Indo-European as follows: "Among the patterns discussed in section 1.4 [entitled "A Syntactic Framework Based on Typological Study"], some are susceptible to rearrangement for marking, such as the basic sentence pattern and the position of adjectives and genitives with regard to their nouns. Others are rearranged with difficulty, such as comparatives. . . . Still other characteristic patterns can be rearranged relatively readily, such as the shift of a postposition to prepositional order, as was common in Classical Sanskrit and Greek. For this reason we ascribe great importance to constructions like the comparative in determining the basic patterns of individual languages. Other patterns, however, often reveal the trend of development in a language if it is undergoing change of a syntactic type. In the course of time, then, marked patterns may become predominant in a language and in this way contribute to its change in basic type" (p. 22).

Perhaps the most serious criticism of typological reconstruction as it has been applied to date, however, is the one implied in a remark of Lightfoot's (1979:156)—although this criticism was not the thrust of the remark in its context—who states, "It is assumed that the protolanguage is a 'consistent' type (for example that Proto-Indo-European is consistently SVO (Friedrich [1975]), SOV (Lehmann [1974]),[2] VSO (Miller [1975])) and that it is progressing along definable lines to another consistent type." As I have stated elsewhere (cf., for example, Costello 1978a:238), one must exercise great caution in employing a method of reconstruction that can produce inconsistent results, as the typological reconstruction of word order patterns apparently has for the above-mentioned linguists. Unlike Lehmann's method, however, the tagmemic approach to syntactic reconstruction as here presented is not susceptible to Birnbaum's second criticism (or to the one implied in Lightfoot's statement) since it does not infer earlier patterns of word order of a protolanguage from word order patterns in daughter languages.

John R. Costello

New York, N.Y.
March 1982

---

2. It is factually incorrect to say that Lehmann assumes that Proto-Indo-European was consistently SOV, as foregoing quotations from his *Proto-Indo-European Syntax* indicate.

Acknowledgments

The basic theses of this work were discussed in my paper entitled "Comparative Reconstruction and the Tagmeme" in March 1979, and the criteria for distinguishing between merger and split were discussed in "The Problem of Differentiation in Linguistic Reconstruction" in March 1980, at successive annual conferences of the International Linguistic Association held at New York University. I benefited greatly from the comments expressed on these occasions.

I would like to thank all of my colleagues and students who have helped me to formulate my ideas with their criticism and discussion: Robert L. and Doris S. Allen, Gur Prit F. Bains, Giuliano Bonfante, Alice Deakins, Peter H. Fries, Robert A. Fowkes, Robert French, Howard Garey, Klaus Hameyer, Louis G. Heller, and James Macris. I am greatly indebted to five individuals and their works, which were constantly consulted during the writing of this book: Walter A. Cook, S.J., Henry M. Hoenigswald, Robert E. Longacre, Evelyn G. Pike, and Kenneth L. Pike. I wish to express my deepest appreciation to Ruth M. Brend for her generous gifts of time and counsel.

Abbreviations and Symbols

adj	Adjective
AffAux	Affirmative auxiliary verb slot
affaux	Affirmative auxiliary verb
AffCl	Affirmative clause
Affirm	Affirmation slot
AffSent	Affirmative sentence
AffV	Affirmative verb phrase
Aux	Auxiliary verb slot
aux	Auxiliary verb
auxnuc	Auxiliary verb nucleus slot
auxst	Auxiliary verb stem
Base	Sentence base slot
Cl	Clause
Conj	Conjugational suffix slot
conj	Conjugational suffix
Decl	Declensional suffix slot
decl	Declensional suffix
DeclarSent	Declarative sentence
Det	Determiner slot
det	Determiner
FinAux	Finite auxiliary verb slot
finaux	Finite auxiliary verb
ImperSent	Imperative sentence
InCl	Intransitive clause
Int	Interrogative particle slot
int	Interrogative particle
InterrSent	Interrogative sentence
InV	Intransitive verb phrase
inv	Intransitive verb
L_1	Daughter language$_1$
L_2	Daughter language$_2$
ModAux	Modal auxiliary verb slot

modaux	Modal auxiliary verb
Modf	Noun modifier slot
N	Noun phrase
n	noun
NAdv	Noun-modifying adverbial
NH	Head of a noun phrase
nnuc	Noun nucleus slot
nst	Noun stem
O	Object slot
OptCl	Optative clause
OptSent	Optative sentence
OptV	Optative verb phrase
P	Predicate slot
Part	Relative particle
PasAux	Passive auxiliary verb slot
pasaux	Passive auxiliary verb
PasCl	Passive clause
PasTrCl	Passive transitive clause
PasTrV	Passive transitive verb phrase
pastrv	Passive transitive verb
PasV	Passive verb phrase
Pn	Pronoun
Pos	Possession slot
prep	Preposition
Q	Question
Reld	Related slot of a relater-related phrase
RelPn	Relative pronoun
Relr	Relater slot of a relater-related phrase
RR	Relater-related phrase
S	Subject slot
SubjSent	Subjunctive sentence
SubjV	Subjunctive verb phrase
TrCl	Transitive clause
TrV	Transitive verb phrase
trv	Transitive verb
v	Verb
VAdv	Verb-modifying adverbial
VH	Head of a verb phrase
:	Indicates that the tagmeme whose function is written to the left of the colon is manifested by the allotagma(s) written to the right of the colon
::	Indicates that (a) the tagmeme whose syntactic function (slot) is written to the left of the double colon is correlated with the syntactosemantic

Abbreviations and Symbols

	function (role) written to the right of the double colon
/	Separates the coallotagmas of a tagmeme and the coallosyntagmas of a syntagmeme
—	Indicates the position of a linguistic element within its environment
∅	Zero
#	Silence
+	Indicates that the following tagmeme is obligatory within an allosyntagma
±	Indicates that the following tagmeme is optional within an allosyntagma
" "	Indicates a tagmeme or a syntagmeme
' '	Indicates (a) an allotagma (or allotagmas); or (b) an allosyntagma (or allosyntagmas)
[ ]	Indicates that the syntagmeme whose label is written to the left of the brackets is manifested by the allosyntagma(s) written within the brackets
. . .	Indicates that additional unspecified emic or etic units are optional

A capital letter may serve as a cover symbol for (a) the slot of a tagmeme, or (b) the label of a syntagmeme.

A lower case letter may serve as a cover symbol for the etic unit manifesting an emic unit.

An arabic numeral may serve as a cover symbol for a contrastive or characteristic environment class.

Introduction

In chapter 1 there is a discussion of the tagmeme, the syntagmeme, and comparative reconstruction. Both the tagmeme and the syntagmeme are viewed synchronically and diachronically, and the notion of contrast as it may most advantageously be employed in comparative reconstruction is discussed. Also, a principle is proposed for reconstructing allotagmas and allosyntagmas under certain conditions.

In chapter 2 patterns of tagmemic and syntagmemic change are discussed and illustrated: one-to-one replacement, merger, split, and their subtypes, including regular change, "semantic change," innovation, and borrowing. Also, there is a discussion of amorphous loss or disappearance, and amorphous gain or increment.

In chapter 3 the methods of comparative reconstruction are applied to instances of each of the tagmemic and syntagmemic changes covered in chapter 2. Also, criteria are established which are designed to enable the linguist to distinguish instances of split from those of merger, and instances of amorphous loss from those of amorphous gain.

In chapter 4 two approaches to tagmemic and syntagmemic syntactosemantic reconstruction are presented, one on the basis of a "syntactic tagmeme," and one on the basis of a "semantic tagmeme."

1 The Tagmeme, the Syntagmeme, and Comparative Reconstruction

In the first two sections of this chapter, the tagmeme and the syntagmeme will be dealt with from a synchronic and a diachronic point of view, with particular attention being given to the notion of contrast as it applies to these emic units. In the third section, fundamental procedures of the comparative method will be related to the tagmeme and the syntagmeme in order to demonstrate the suitability of these units in comparative reconstruction.

1.1 The Tagmeme[1]

1.1.1. The Tagmeme Viewed Synchronically. As defined by Longacre (1964:15f.), the tagmeme is "a functional point (not necessarily a point in a fixed linear sequence) at which a set of items and/or sequences occur." Cook (1969:15) elaborates as follows, "Functional slots are positions in construction frames which define the role of linguistic forms [i.e., fillers or allotagmas] in the construction relative to other points of the same construction." Thus, according to Cook, "functions are grammatical relationships." It is worthy of note that the notions of *function* and *filler* underlying the tagmeme were recognized and contrasted at least as early as 1660 by Arnauld and Lancelot in the *Port-Royal Grammar*. For example, in part 2, chapter 6 of that work, the authors preface their observations on substantival function as follows: "If one always considered things separately from one another, one would only have given to nouns two modifications that we have just indicated, namely number for all sorts of nouns, and gender for adjectives. But because they are often considered in terms of the

---

1. As was stated in the preface, Pike and Pike (1982) have defined the tagmeme as having four cells: *slot* (syntactic function), *class* (a linguistic form or filler), *role* (a semantic function), and *cohesion* (agreement in number, gender, case, etc.). Of these, only slot and class will be treated, with the exception that role will be dealt with in 2.2.1.1 (et passim) in examples dealing with levels of grammar above the sentence, and in chapter 4.

1

different relationships which they have with one another, one of the inventions which was made in order to mark these relationships was to give different endings to nouns . . ." (p. 79).[2] The authors then list, discuss, and illustrate these relationships, and later (part 2, chapter 6) extend the list of items which signal these functions to include prepositions, "We have said above in Chapter VI that cases and prepositions have been invented for the same purpose, namely, to indicate the relationship which things have to one another" (p. 115).

It is furthermore noteworthy that phenomena that prompted tagmemicists to make statements such as, "So intimate is the correlativity of function and set that each is mutually dependent on the other; the function cannot exist apart from the set nor has the set significance apart from the function" (Longacre 1964:15), were recognized also by Arnauld and Lancelot, who described the imperfect signalling of substantival function as follows: "First, on the subject of prepositions, no language has followed what reason would have desired, which is that one relationship should be marked by one preposition, and that the same preposition should only mark one relationship. For, on the contrary, what we have seen in the above examples taken from French happens in all languages, namely that the identical relationship is signified by several prepositions, as *dans, en, à* can all signify [the relationship] *in;* and that the same preposition, like *en* or *à,* mark different relationships" (pp. 117f.). Strangely enough, it was to take almost three hundred years until the problem of the misalignment of function and its signification observed by Arnauld and Lancelot was resolved in a linguistic unit called the tagmeme (originally named the grameme) by Pike (1954, 1958).

It is a well-established practice in comparative reconstruction (implicit, for example, in almost every diagram of Hoenigswald 1960) to define contrast between emic units (in particular, the phoneme and the morpheme) on the basis of *distribution* rather than that of *feature* or *manifestation mode,* and for this reason it is desirable to be able to demonstrate contrast between tagmemes[3] in a fashion parallel to the way that one determines contrast between morphemes, linguistic units related to tagmemes. The tagmeme shares with the morpheme the

---

2. I do not subscribe to the view of the origin of linguistic elements implied in this passage.

3. The present work approaches tagmemic contrast from the point of view of *distribution,* which is most suitable for the operations of comparative reconstruction. See Pike (1972:170, note 18 et passim) for discussion of the notions *feature mode, manifestation mode,* and *distribution mode.* See Pike (1959) and Algeo (1974:4) for discussion of the related concepts *particle, wave,* and *field,* respectively, and Heller and Macris (1979) for a discussion of *reactance,* a concept closely allied to contrast.

property of being a linguistic unit that links content and expression. As far as content is concerned, the morpheme conveys a root, derivational, or inflectional concept, whereas the tagmeme represents a syntactic or a syntactosemantic function. As far as expression is concerned, on the other hand, the morphs which realize morphemes are often not homonymous (some languages, like Chinese, however, provide many exceptions to this statement), whereas the fillers or allotagmas of different tagmemes often are, e.g., S:N/Pn/Cl . . ., O:N/Pn/Cl. . . . Because it is essential to be able to account for contrast among tagmemes whether they are homonymous or not, the ensuing discussion will cover homonymous as well as nonhomonymous tagmemes. For purposes of illustration, let the allotagma N of the tagmeme S:N . . . be represented as a_1, the allotagma N of the tagmeme O:N . . . as a_2,[4] and the allotagma TrV of the tagmeme P:TrV as b (thus following the custom in discussions on morphemics of indicating only the allomorph of a morpheme, and leaving the content of the morpheme to be expressed according to the distribution of the allomorph). Just as one may differentiate the contrastive and characteristic sets of environments for morphemes (cf. Hoenigswald 1960:15, 28, fig. 7) one may also differentiate these environments for tagmemes. Following Hoenigswald, one may thus label the contrastive set of environments (including at least the minimum frame #__#) for a_1, a_2, and b, as 1, and the characteristic sets of environments for these tagmemes as 2, 3, and 4, respectively; diagrammatically, then, the emic status, as well as the content of each tagmeme, is indicated as in figure 1 (cf. Hoenigswald 1960:15f.).

	1	2	3	4
a_1	x	x	-	-
a_2	x	-	x	-
b	x	-	-	x

Fig. 1

Thus, just as one determines that homonymous morphs belong to different morphemes if they are distributed over separate sets of characteristic environments (cf. Hoenigswald 1960:18f.), one may also

---

4. Other coallotagmas of S: and O: have been omitted in the interest of clarity in presentation.

determine that homonymous tagmas manifest separate tagmemes on this same basis.[5] It will be seen in 1.4 that it is precisely because it is possible to establish contrast between tagmemes that comparative reconstruction may be applied to corresponding sets of tagmemes in two daughter languages to reconstruct prototagmemes in a parent language, even (in an abstract sense) independently of the syntagmemes in which they occur.

1.1.2. The Tagmeme Viewed Diachronically. In the preceding section, the tagmeme was viewed synchronically. Like the morpheme, the tagmeme may also be viewed diachronically. Since tagmemic notation normally indicates a function and the item or items (allotagmas) manifesting that function simultaneously, let A:a and B:b represent two tagmemes in the earlier stage of a language, and let M:a and N:b represent tagmemes at the later stage, where a capital letter symbolizes a function, and a lower case letter symbolizes an allotagma. In a one-to-one replacement pattern (cf. fig. 2), M:a occurs in the same environments in which A:a occurred, and N:b occurs in the same environments in which B:b occurred; in other words, M:a replaces A:a, and N:b replaces B:b.

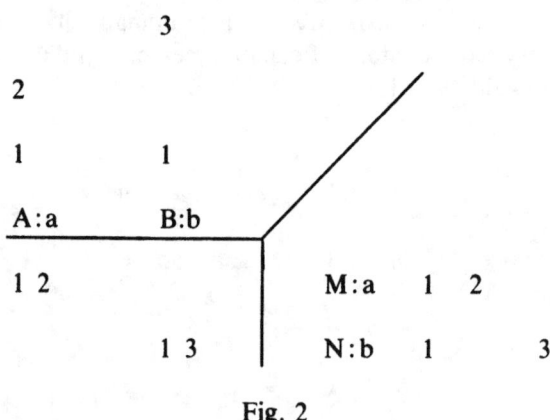

Fig. 2

To paraphrase Hoenigswald (1960:27), the choice of different function symbols for different stages in diachronic diagrams such as figure 2

---

5. Hoenigswald (1960:64, note 8) observes that "the contrastive environment, at least in [morphemic] homonyms, may also be characterized as an AMBIGUOUS environment." This is equally true for tagmemic homonyms.

recalls the fact that emic units are defined synchronically, that is, by all other emic units of the same stage of a language. In the interest of clarity, however, it is advantageous to use identical lower case symbols to indicate instances when allotagmas between two stages are unchanged; in chapters 2 and 3 it will be seen that this is a necessity, since various subtypes of one-to-one replacement, merger, and split are distinguished allotagmatically. In practice, and for the same reason, Hoenigswald (1960, figs. 8, 9, 12, 14b, 17, 18, 27, 29, 32, and 39) has employed a parallel notation in illustrating morphological change. Also, as Hoenigswald notes, different sets of numerals should be used to indicate that environment classes between two stages are corresponding rather than identical; in the interest of simplicity, however, I follow Hoenigswald (1960) in employing the same set of numerals to indicate corresponding environments between the earlier and later stage.[6] Thus in the three-dimensional diagram of figure 2, A:a and B:b together with their environment sets appear on the horizontal axis, which is reserved for tagmemes of the earlier stage, and M:a and N:b, together with their environment sets, appear on the vertical axis, which is reserved for tagmemes of the later stage. The numerals appearing in the area bounded by the horizontal and vertical axes, an intermediate stage, are placed at intersections linking the earlier tagmemes with their replacements, environment by environment.

1.2 The Syntagmeme

1.2.1. The Syntagmeme Viewed Synchronically. A construction the constituents of which are tagmemes is called a syntagmeme. According to Longacre (1965:70), "... a syntagmeme is a structurally contrastive type on a given level of hierarchical structuring; e.g. a word type (in terms of internal structure), a phrase type, a clause type, a sentence type, a paragraph type, a discourse type."

If the syntagmeme is viewed as a unit rather than as a collective sequence of consituents, it is possible to establish contrast[7] between these units on the basis of the environments that they occupy.

---

6. Hoenigswald (1973:1) proposes a solution to this problem by labelling environments in the early period of a language as 1, 2, 3, etc., and the corresponding environments in the later period as 101, 102, 103, etc.; however, I find this impractical for the large number of diagrams to be presented.

7. Bearing in mind the operations established for comparative reconstruction, I present here a framework for determining contrast among syntagmemes that is based upon the notion of *distribution mode*. See Longacre (1966, especially pp. 251f.) and Pike (1972:170ff.) for additional details and discussion of syntagmemic contrast.

Following the treatment of tagmemes, let the allosyntagma of the syntagmeme N = +Det:det +NH:n be represented as a, and let the allosyntagma of the syntagmeme TrV = +VH:trv be represented as b. Also, let the contrastive set of environments (including at least the minimum frame #__#) of these syntagmemes be labelled as 1, and the characteristic set of environments be labelled as 2 and 3, respectively, where the syntagmemes are constituents of constructions in which they are included (cf. Hoenigswald 1960:15f.). Now the emic status, as well as the content of each syntagmeme is indicated diagrammatically as in figure 3.

```
         1    2    3

    a    x    x    -

    b    x    -    x
```

Fig. 3

It will be seen in 1.4 that just as in the case of the tagmeme, it is the contrastive property of the syntagmeme that enables us to retrieve protosyntagmemes via the operations of comparative reconstruction.

1.2.2. The Syntagmeme Viewed Diachronically. Just as is the case with the morpheme and the tagmeme, the syntagmeme may also be viewed diachronically. Typically, the formula of a syntagmeme is written in such a way that the label of the construction is followed by an equals sign, which in turn is followed by the string of constituents that make up the construction (as in 1.2.1). Recently, however, Hale (1976:63 and 84, note 14) has employed a variant formulation for syntagmemes, where the constituents of the construction are enclosed in brackets, and the label of the construction appears immediately to the left of the initial bracket. One of the advantages of this notation is that it facilitates keeping track of adjacent and included syntagmemes when one analyzes long complex sentences. Moreover, such formulae may easily be converted into tagmemic tree diagrams, where the label of the syntagmeme is indicated as a node, and the constituents are indicated as branches from that node; thus brackets indicate a shift from one grammatical level to another. For these reasons, Hale's bracketing notation will be employed in the remainder of this work. By way of illustration, let A[a] and B[b] represent syntagmemes in the earlier

Comparative Reconstruction

stage of a language, and let M[a] and N[b] represent syntagmemes at the later stage, where a capital letter symbolizes the label of a syntagmeme, and a lower case letter symbolizes an allosyntagma. In a one-to-one replacement pattern (fig. 4), M[a] occurs in the same environments in which A[a] occurred, and N[b] occurs in the same environments in which B[b] occurred; in other words, M[a] replaces A[a], and N[b] replaces B[b].

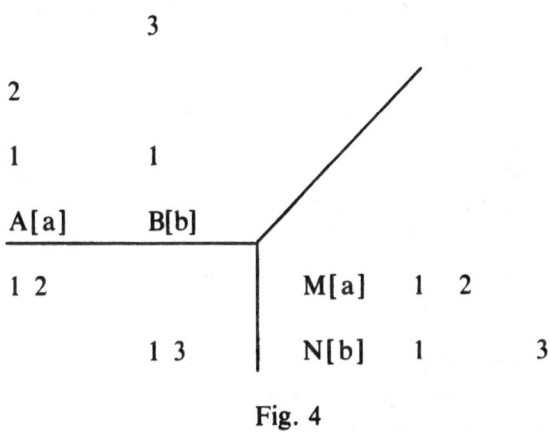

Fig. 4

The reasons that different constructional labels for different stages are chosen, whereas identical numerals and identical lower case symbols are used to indicate corresponding environment sets and allosyntagmas, respectively, for different stages, are the same as those mentioned in 1.1.2 in connection with tagmemic function symbols, environment sets, and allotagmas. Thus, just like the tagmemes in figure 2, the syntagmemes A[a] and B[b] in figure 4, together with their environment sets, appear on the horizontal axis, and M[a] and N[b], together with their environment sets, appear on the vertical axis. Also, the numerals appearing in the intermediate stage, which is framed by the horizontal and vertical axes, are placed at intersections linking earlier syntagmemes with their replacements, environment by environment.

1.3 Excursus: Horizontal and Vertical Etic Units

It is possible to distinguish between two kinds of etic units for tagmemes and syntagmemes: horizontal etic units, which are variants on the level at which the emic unit is manifested, and vertical etic units, which are variants on some level below that at which the emic unit is manifested.[8]

As was indicated in the preceding paragraph, horizontal coallotagmas and coallosyntagmas occur on the level at which the emic unit with which they are associated is manifested. Horizontal coallotagmas of a tagmeme are observed when a tagmeme has more than one filler. For example, 'S:N' and 'S:Pn' are horizontal coallotagmas of the "S:N/Pn/Cl . . ." tagmeme. (A convention is introduced here whereby double quotation marks are employed to indicate an emic unit, and single quotation marks, an etic member of an emic unit.) Horizontal coallosyntagmas are of two types: those which involve two or more arrangements of the same constituents of the syntagmeme, and those which involve additions or deletions of the constituents, all on the same level. An example of coallosyntagmas of the first type would be 'TrCl [+S:N +P:TrV +O:N]' and 'TrCl [+O:N +P:TrV +S:N]'. An example of coallosyntagmas of the second type would be 'TrCl [+S:N +P:TrV +O:N]' and 'TrCl [+S:N +P:TrV +VAdv:RR]'. For a case in phonology similar to the latter example, consider utterance-long elements of intonation on the suprasegmental phonemic level. In a discussion of these, Harris (1951:56) writes ". . . the difference between *0100120 (The fellow out there fumbled.)* and *120 (I fumbled.)* correlates with the difference in number and position of loud and zero stressed vowels. Following the method of 7.3 and 10.4, we may group all the contours that consist of various 1's and 0's followed by a final 20, and list them as positional variants of one contour *-20*." Put somewhat differently, *0100120* and *120* (and all other contours that consist of various 1's and 0's followed by a final 20) are horizontal suprasegmental coallomorphs of a suprasegmental morpheme *-20*.

As was indicated above, vertical coallotagmas and coallosyntagmas occur on some level below that at which the emic unit with which they are associated is manifested. Vertical coallotagmas are observed when a filler of a tagmeme is expanded by more than one coallosyntagma of a syntagmeme on a lower level; for example, 'P:TrV [+VH:trv]' and 'P:TrV [+Aux:aux +VH:trv]' are vertical coallotagmas of "P:TrV". For a similar case in phonology, consider the suprasegmental phoneme /+/, open transition, in American English.[9] According to Gleason (1961:43), "When /+/ follows immediately after a syllable nucleus, as in *slyness*, it is expressed [i.e., manifested—JC], in part, by a prolongation of the syllable nucleus. . . . After certain consonants, notably /m n ŋ/, it is expressed by prolongation of the preceding consonant. After some other consonants it takes the form of a weakening of the voicing.

---

8. See Pike and Pike (1977:26) for a similar use of the terms *horizontal* and *vertical*.

9. I am indebted to Ruth M. Brend (personal communication) for this observation.

After voiceless stops it is shown by contrasts in the degree of aspiration. /+/ also has certain noticeable effects on the following vowel or consonant. In short, in a pair like *night rate* and *nitrate,* though a native speaker interprets the facts as a break or even a very short pause between *night* and *rate,* the differences are actually in the details of pronunciation of both the /t/ and the /r/." In other words, the suprasegmental phoneme /+/ has vertical coallophones on the segmental phonetic level. Vertical coallosyntagmas are observed when a constituent of a syntagmeme is expanded by more than one coallosyntagma of a syntagmeme on a lower level; for example, 'TrCl [+S:N +P:TrV [+VH:trv] +O:N]' and 'TrCl [+S:N +P:TrV [+Aux:aux +VH:trv] +O:N]' are vertical coallosyntagmas of "TrCl [+S:N +P:TrV +O:N]".

1.4 Comparative Reconstruction

In his essay "The Problem of Linguistic Subgrouping," Greenberg (1957:49) expressed an axiom which underlies all comparative reconstruction, "occurrence in at least two separate branches of a family is the common reason for assigning a feature to the ancestral language of the family as a whole."[10] In the following statement, Hoenigswald (1960:132) relates this axiom specifically to the reconstruction of phonemes, "The comparative method [with the goal of achieving protophonemes] is based on the principle that sets of recurring phoneme correspondences between two related languages continue blocks of positional allophones [i.e., protophonemes] from the mother language; therefore, if such sets are subjected to the treatment accorded to phones in synchronic phonemics, a reconstruction is obtained." That this axiom may be applied successfully to the reconstruction of another emic unit, the morpheme, has also been demonstrated by Hoenigswald (1960:70f.). It is the objective of the present work to show that this axiom is applicable to the reconstruction of tagmemes and syntagmemes as well.

Paraphrasing in general terms the relationship between elements in the parent and daughter languages which makes it possible to reconstruct phonemes (and morphemes), we may say that if an emic unit A of the ancestor language appears as an emic unit M in one daughter language and as an emic unit T in another daughter language, corresponding strings in the two sister languages will be matched in such a way that M in one answers to T in the other. Such a pair of emic units,

---

10. It was with this axiom in mind that I have assigned features (in the broadest sense of the word) like accusative substantival adverb of direction, instrumental substantival adverb of means, etc., to Proto-Indo-European on the basis of their distribution in Indic, Hellenic, Baltic, and other branches of the Indo-European family (cf. Costello 1975).

one in the first language and one in the other, is a set of correspondences, written T/M. This may be expressed diagrammatically in terms of the reconstruction diagram in figure 5 (cf. Hoenigswald 1960:119).

		1 2	T	1 2	Daughter Language$_1$
Proto-Language	A 1 2				
		1 2	M	1 2	Daughter Language$_2$

Fig. 5

If the preceding paraphrase is correct, then the following principle holds in comparative tagmemic and comparative syntagmemic reconstruction:

> Sets of correspondences of tagmemes and syntagmemes between two daughter languages may be considered to be continuations of respective prototagmemes and protosyntagmemes in the parent language, just as sets of correspondences of phonemes and morphemes between two daughter languages may be considered to be continuations of respective protophonemes and protomorphemes in the parent language.

To be sure, etic units are defined in comparative phonemic reconstruction primarily (and in comparative morphemic reconstruction exclusively) from the point of view of distribution rather than manifestation mode (cf. Hoenigswald 1960:70, note 4, and 134–37).[11] For that reason, and because merger is the central process of change involving phonemes (and morphemes), it is possible, under conditions such as certain reassignments without merger, and even unconditional merger in one of two daughter languages (cf. Hoenigswald 1960:121, 127) to assign etic units—albeit from the point of view of distribution, not manifestation—to protoemic units even when the environments of these etic units are not parallel in the daughter languages concerned. Regarding tagmemes and syntagmemes, however, etic units are defined essentially from the point of view of manifestation mode. Because of this, the following principle is proposed for etic units in comparative tagmemic and comparative syntagmemic reconstruction:

---

11. Certainly this is not true, however, with respect to viewing phonemic (and morphemic) change (cf. Hoenigswald 1960:87, 9.1.1; 93f., 9.2.1).

No etic characteristics of emic units aside from those that are distributed in each of the daughter languages involved in a reconstruction should be assigned to the protoemic units of the parent language.

2 Tagmemic and Syntagmemic Change

In this chapter the types of change that have been observed between morphemes and allomorphs of one stage of a language and another—one-to-one replacement, merger, split, amorphous loss, and amorphous emergence—will be dealt with as they affect tagmemes, syntagmemes, allotagmas, and allosyntagmas. Since identical replacement patterns apply to (a) syntagmemes as well as tagmemes, (b) allosyntagmas as well as allotagmas, and (c) a number of etic members as well as the emic units to which they belong, one diagram will frequently be referred to for several of the emic and etic changes to be discussed. For this reason, only capital letters, which refer to emic units, and lower case letters, which refer to etic members of emic units, will be found in the diagrams. Consequently the interpretation of a capital letter will vary, being either a tagmemic function or a syntagmemic label, depending upon the context of the discussion in which reference to it is made. Likewise the interpretation of a lower case letter will vary, being either an allotagma or an allosyntagma, also depending upon the context of the discussion in which reference to it is made. In the actual discussion of the linguistic changes, however, colons and brackets will be used to indicate tagmemes and syntagmemes, respectively, as in 1.1.2 and 1.2.2; moreover, as was indicated in 1.3, a convention is introduced in the present work whereby double quotation marks are employed to designate an emic unit, and single quotation marks, an etic member of an emic unit.

2.1 One-to-one Replacement

In one-to-one replacement, one emic unit of the earlier stage is replaced in each of its environments by one emic unit in the later stage, in corresponding environments. Likewise, one etic member of an emic unit of the earlier stage is replaced in each of its environments by one etic unit in the later stage, in corresponding environments. The four subtypes of this replacement pattern, regular replacement, replacement by semantic change,[1] replacement by innovation, and replacement by borrowing, will be discussed in turn.

2.1.1. Regular Replacement. In this subtype of one-to-one replacement, the etic member (or members) belonging to an emic unit of the later stage is identical to the etic member (or members) belonging to the corresponding emic unit of the earlier stage.

2.1.1.1. Tagmemic. The tagmeme "A:a" is replaced by "M:a" in 1^2 and 2, and "B:b" is replaced by "N:b" in 1 and 3 (fig. 6).

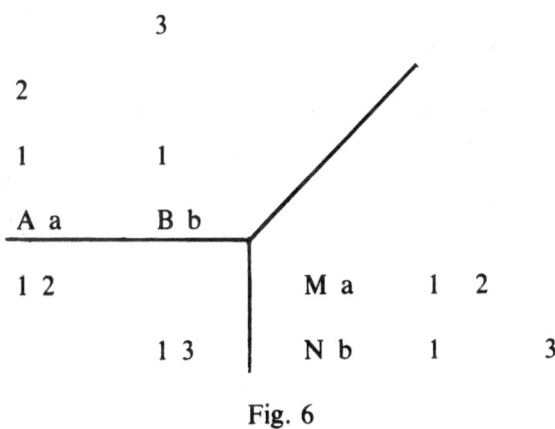

Fig. 6

Neither merger nor split is involved. Such a replacement pattern is found among constituents of the noun phrase between Middle English (ME) and Modern English (NE ["New English"]). For example, ME "Modf:adj" and "NH:n" are replaced by NE "Modf:adj" and "NH:n", respectively, where 1 is the contrastive set, 2, characteristic for "Modf:adj", includes N [±Det:det__ +NH:n], and 3, characteristic

---

1. The term *semantic change*, which is technically appropriate only with respect to particular subtypes of morphological replacement patterns, is employed throughout this work in reference to certain subtypes of tagmemic and syntagmemic replacement patterns which are parallel to semantic change in morphology (cf., for example, 2.1.2, 2.2.2, and 2.3.2).

2. Arabic numerals refer to environment sets. Throughout the present work, it is assumed that 1 includes the minimal frame #__# (cf. Hoenigswald 1960:16, 24 note 22, and 64 note 8).

for 'NH:n'', includes N [±Det:det ±Modf:adj__]. The functions of "A:a" and "B:b" have remained constant between the earlier stage and the later stage. In terms of the immediately preceding example of the noun phrase in English (E), the functions of "Modf:adj" and "NH:n" have remained constant between Middle English and Modern English.

2.1.1.2. Syntagmemic. The syntagmeme "A[a]" is replaced by "M[a]" in 1 and 2, and "B[b]" is replaced by "N[b]" in 1 and 3 (cf. fig. 6). Such a replacement pattern is found among transitive and intransitive verb phrases between Middle English and Modern English. For example, ME "TrV [+ModAux:modaux +VH:trv]" and "InV [+ModAux:modaux +VH:inv]" are replaced by themselves, respectively, in Modern English, where 1 is the contrastive set, 2, characteristic for "TrV [. . .]", includes TrCl [±S: . . . +P:__ +O: . . .], and 3, characteristic for "InV [. . .]", includes InCl [+S: . . . +P:__ . . .]. Both "A[a]" and its replacement "M[a]", and "B[b]" and its replacement "N[b]", have remained constant in their usage as constructional types between the earlier stage and the later stage. In terms of the immediately preceding example, the uses of "TrV [. . .]" and "InV [. . .]" have remained constant between Middle English and Modern English.

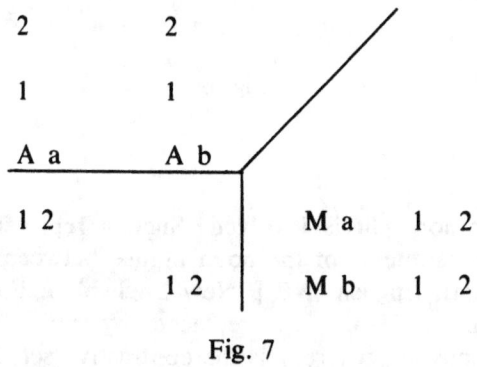

Fig. 7

2.1.1.3 Allotagmatic.[3] The specific allotagmas 'A:a' and 'A:b' of the tagmeme "A:a/b" are replaced by 'M:a' and 'M:b', respectively, in 1

---

3. In a discussion of emic change, the primary concerns are (a) the replacement pattern of the function(s) or constructional type(s) involved; and (b) the replacement pattern of the total set of etic units that manifest the function(s) or constructional type(s). In a discussion of etic change, on the other hand, the *emphasis* is on the replacement pattern of selected etic members of the total set manifesting an emic function or constructional type. This important distinction may be obscured in examples of both kinds of change, emic and etic, in which only a small number of etic elements are treated.

and 2 (fig. 7). Neither merger nor split is involved. Such a replacement pattern is found among the allotagmas of the Subject tagmeme between Middle English and Modern English. For example, ME 'S:N' and 'S:Pn' are replaced by NE 'S:N' and 'S:Pn', respectively, where 1 is the contrastive set, and 2, characteristic for "S:N/Pn . . .", includes Cl [__ +P: . . .].

2.1.1.4. Allosyntagmatic.[4] The allosyntagmas 'A[a]' and 'A[b]' are replaced by 'M[a]' and 'M[b]', respectively, in 1 and 2 (cf. fig. 7). Such a replacement pattern is found among the allosyntagmas of the noun phrase between Middle English and Modern English. For example, the Middle English allosyntagmas 'N [+Det:det +NH:n]' and 'N [+Det:det +Modf:adj +NH:n]' are replaced by themselves, respectively, in Modern English, where 1 is the contrastive set, and 2, characteristic for "N [. . .]", includes Cl [+S:__ . . .].

2.1.2. Replacement with Semantic Change. As in morphemic semantic change, so also in tagmemic and syntagmemic change, the etic member (or members) belonging to an emic unit of the later stage is identical to the etic member (or members) belonging to a noncorresponding emic unit of the earlier stage (cf. footnote 1).

2.1.2.1. Tagmemic. The tagmeme "A:a" is replaced by "M:b" in 1 and 2, and "B:b" is replaced by "N:c" in 1 and 3 (fig. 8).

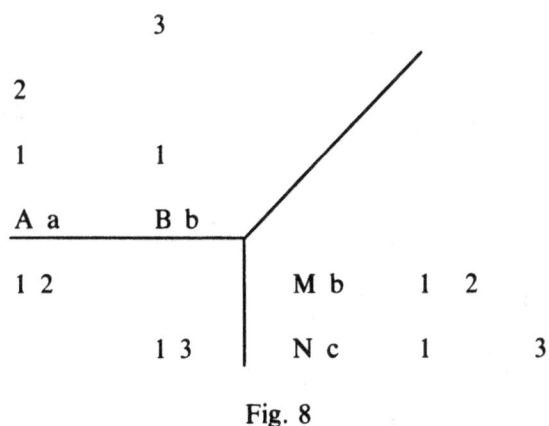

Fig. 8

---

4. See footnote 3.

Thus, the allotagma associated with "A:a" is replaced in the later stage by the allotagma that was formerly associated with "B:b". The provenience of the allotagma of "N:c" is of no concern here. In this subtype of one-to-one replacement, "M:b" is functionally equivalent to "A:a". However, since the filler "M:b" was once associated with another tagmeme, "B:b", this is a tagmemic parallel of semantic change in morphology.

2.1.2.2. Syntagmemic. The syntagmeme "A[a]" is replaced by "M[b]" in 1 and 2, and "B[b]" is replaced by "N[c]" in 1 and 3 (cf. fig. 8). Although the allosyntagma of "M[b]" was formerly associated with "B[b]", rather than "A[a]", "M[b]" is, as a constructional type, equivalent to "A[a]". Thus, this is a syntagmemic parallel of semantic change in morphology. The origin of the allosyntagma of "N[c]" is not relevant to the change under discussion.

2.1.2.3. Allotagmatic. The allotagma 'A:a' is replaced by 'M:b' in 1 and 2, and 'B:b' is replaced by 'N:c' in 1 and 3; thus an allotagma that was associated with one tagmeme in the earlier stage is associated with a different (contrastive) tagmeme in the later stage (cf. fig. 8). The source of the allotagma 'N:c' is of no concern in this pattern of change.

2.1.2.4 Allosyntagmatic. The allosyntagma 'A[a]' in 1 and 2 and 'B[b]' in 1 and 3 are represented by 'M[b]' and 'N[c]' in corresponding environments in the later stage; thus an allosyntagma that was associated with one constructional type in the earlier stage is associated with another (contrastive) type in the later stage (cf. fig. 8).

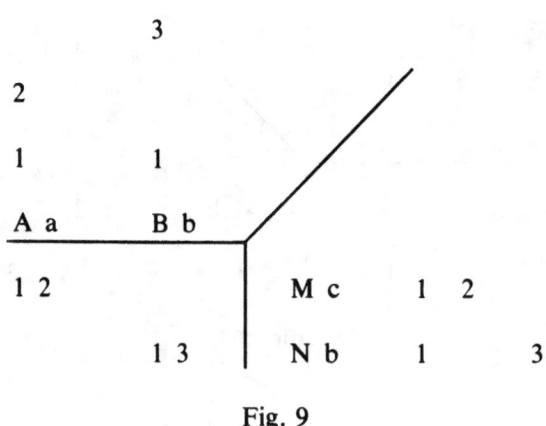

Fig. 9

2.1.3. Replacement with Innovation.
In this subtype of one-to-one replacement, the etic member (or members) belonging to an emic unit of the earlier stage is replaced by an etic member in the later stage that did not occur anywhere in the earlier stage.

2.1.3.1. Tagmemic. The tagmeme "A:a" is replaced by "M:c" in 1 and 2 (and "B:b" is replaced by "N:b" in 1 and 3) (fig. 9). The allotagma which manifested "A:a" is replaced in the later stage by an allotagma that entered the language by innovation. (The replacement of "B:b" by "N:b" is regular, and is included in figure 9 only for the sake of contrast with replacement by innovation.) In this subtype of one-to-one replacement, "M:c" is functionally equivalent to "A:a". Since the filler of "M:c" was introduced into the language as an innovation, this is an example of a tagmemic parallel of replacement by innovation in morphology.

2.1.3.2. Syntagmemic. The syntagmeme "A[a]" is replaced by "M[c]" in 1 and 2 (and "B[b]" is replaced by "N[b]" in 1 and 3)(cf. fig. 9). The allosyntagma associated with "A[a]" is replaced in the later stage by an allosyntagma that was introduced into the language as an innovation. (The regular replacement of "B[b]" by "N[b]" is included only as a contrast with replacement by innovation.) Although the allosyntagma of "M[c]" was not associated with any syntagmeme in the earlier stage, "M[c]" is equivalent to "A[a]". Thus, this is a syntagmemic parallel of one-to-one replacement in morphology.

2.1.3.3. Allotagmatic. The allotagma 'A:a' is replaced by 'M:c' in 1 and 2 (and 'B:b' is replaced by 'N:b' in 1 and 3); thus a filler that was associated with a tagmeme in the earlier stage is replaced by a filler that was introduced into the language by innovation (cf. fig. 9).

2.1.3.4. Allosyntagmatic. The allosyntagma 'A[a]' in 1 and 2 is represented by 'M[c]' in corresponding environments in the later stage (and 'B[b]' in 1 and 3 is represented by 'N[b]' in corresponding environments in the later stage)(cf. fig. 9). The allosyntagma 'M[c]' was introduced into the later stage of the language as an innovation. Such a replacement pattern is found between Classical Latin (CL) and Vulgar Latin (VL) in the present tense allosyntagma of the transitive passive verb phrase; thus the Classical Latin syntagmeme in (1)(a) is replaced by the Vulgar Latin syntagmeme in (2)(a), where 1 is the contrastive set and 2, characteristic for "PasTrV", includes PasTrCl [+S: ... +P:__ ...].

(1)(a) 'PasTrV [. . . +VH:pastrv]'
(b) *Pueri servantur* "The boys are saved"

(2)(a) 'PasTrV [. . . +PasAux:pasaux +VH:v]'
(b) *Ut familia nostra bene conservata sit* "That our family be well preserved" (Muller and Taylor 1932:68, 248 line 1)

2.1.4. Replacement with Borrowing. In this subtype of one-to-one replacement, the etic member (or members) belonging to an emic unit of the later stage originates in a foreign language; it may be borrowed with or without modifications.

2.1.4.1. Tagmemic. The tagmeme "A:a" is replaced by "M:c" in 1 and 2 (and "B:b" is replaced by "N:b" in 1 and 3)(cf. fig. 9). The allotagma which manifested "A:a" is replaced in the later stage by an allotagma that entered the language by borrowing from another language. (The replacement of "B:b" by "N:b" is a regular one, and is included here only to show the contrast between replacement by borrowing and regular replacement.) Although the filler of "M:c" was borrowed into the language from another language, "M:c" is functionally equivalent to "A:a", and thus this is a tagmemic parallel of replacement by borrowing in morphology.

2.1.4.2. Syntagmemic. The syntagmeme "A[a]" is replaced by "M[c]" in 1 and 2 (and "B[b]" is replaced by "N[b]" in 1 and 3)(cf. fig. 9). The allosyntagma which manifested "A[a]" is replaced in the later stage by an allosyntagma that came into the language as a calque. (The replacement of "B[b]" by "N[b]", which is regular, merely provides contrast with the present example of replacement with borrowing.) As a borrowing in the later stage, the allosyntagma of "M[c]" is not associated with any syntagmeme in the earlier stage; nevertheless, "M[c]" is equivalent to "A[a]" in that it fills environments that correspond to those that "A[a]" filled. Therefore this is a syntagmemic parallel of one-to-one replacement with borrowing in morphology.

2.1.4.3. Allotagmatic. The specific allotagma 'A:a' of the tagmeme "A: . . ." is replaced by 'M:c' in 1 and 2 (and 'B:b' is replaced by 'N:b' in 1 and 3), where the replacing allotagma was borrowed from a foreign language (cf. fig. 9). Such a replacement pattern is found between older Pennsylvania German (PG) and a contemporary variety of Pennsylvania German, Southeastern Pennsylvania German (SPG). For example, the allotagma in (3)(a) is replaced by the allotagma (from English) in (4)(a), where 1 is the contrastive set, and 2, characteristic for "PasAux:pasaux", includes PasV [. . . __ +VH:v].

(3)(a) 'PasAux:pasaux$_{(native)}$ [+auxnuc:auxst +Conj:conj]'
(b) *Die Gleeder warre vun sellre Fraa gmacht.* "The clothes are (being) made by that woman" (Costello 1978b:32).

Tagmemic and Syntagmemic Change

(4)(a) 'PasAux:pasaux$_{(foreign)}$ [+auxnuc$_{(calque)}$:auxst +Conj:conj]'
(b) *Der Pitscher iss verbroche bei der Anna.* "The pitcher is (being) broken by Anna" (Costello 1978b:32).

2.1.4.4. Allosyntagmatic. The specific allosyntagma 'A[a]' of the syntagmeme "A [...]" is replaced by 'M[c]' in 1 and 2, where the replacing allosyntagma was borrowed from a foreign language (cf. fig. 9). Such a replacement pattern is found between older Pennsylvania German and Southeastern Pennsylvania German. For example, the native passive allosyntagma in (5) is replaced by the allosyntagma (from English) in (6), where 1 is the contrastive set, and 2, characteristic for "PasV [...]", includes PasTrCl [+S: ... +P:___ ...]; cf. (3)(a-b) and (4)(a-b) for details and illustrations.

(5) 'PasTrV [+PasAux:pasaux$_{(native)}$ +VH:v]'

(6) 'PasTrV [+PasAux:pasaux$_{(foreign)}$ +VH:v]'

It is worthy of note to mention that the optional Pennsylvania German transformation that applies to (3)(a) to move the past participle of the verb to clause-final position (as seen in [3] [b]), is not found under the corresponding conditions in Southeastern Pennsylvania German, as witnessed in (4)(b). If the absence of this transformation is, along with the presence of the foreign filler of "PasAux: . . .", a result of the influence of English in Southeastern Pennsylvania German, as has been suggested elsewhere (cf. Costello 1978b:33f.), then this would be an additional characteristic that would distinguish the allosyntagma derived in (3)(a) from the allosyntagma derived in (4)(a).

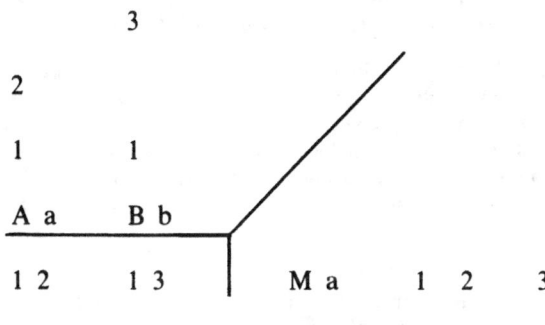

Fig. 10

2.2 Merger

In merger, two or more emic units of the earlier stage are replaced in each of their environments by one emic unit in the later stage, in corresponding environments; likewise, two or more etic members of an emic unit of the earlier stage are replaced in each of their environments by one etic unit in the later stage, in corresponding environments. The four subtypes of this replacement pattern, which are the same as those of one-to-one replacement, will be discussed directly.

2.2.1. Regular Replacement[5]

2.2.1.1. Tagmemic.
The tagmemes "A:a" in 1 and 2, and "B:b" in 1 and 3, are replaced by "M:a" in 1, 2, and 3 (fig. 10). In other words, a merger or loss of contrast has taken place between "A:a" and "B:b". Such a replacement pattern is found in the merger of the Wish (optative) and Volition (subjunctive) tagmemes between Proto-Indo-European (PIE) and Germanic (Gmc.).[6] In other words, Proto-Indo-European "Wish:OptSent" and "Volition:SubjSent"[7] are replaced by Gmc. "Wish:OptSent",[8] where 1 is the contrastive set, 2, characteristic for "Wish:OptSent", includes (Horatory) Discourse [. . . +Prayer: Paragraph [+Invocation: . . . ___ . . . +Credo: . . .] . . .], and 3, characteristic for "Volition:SubjSent", includes (Narrative) Discourse [. . . +Episode:Paragraph [. . . +Q:InterrSent . . . ___ . . .] . . .] (cf. Longacre 1976, and Klammer and Compton 1974).

---

5. Cf. 2.1.1.

6. Cf. Krahe 1965:93: "An *Modi* ("Aussageweisen") besass das Idg. fünf: a) einen *Indikativ* . . . b) einen *Konjunktiv* zum Ausdruck des Willens oder der Bestimmtheit, c) einen *Optativ* als Ausdruck des Wunsches oder der Möglichkeit, d) einen *Imperativ* . . . e) einen . . . *Injunktiv*. Von diesen behielt das Germ. den Indikativ, den Optativ (der die *Funktion* [italics mine—JC] des Konjunktivs und teilweise auch des Imperativs mit übernahm) und den Imperativ. . . ." Also cf. Prokosch 1939:208: "In Germanic . . . the IE [Indo-European] subjunctive [conjugation] disappeared; the so-called present subjunctive is an optative [conjugation] of the present stem. . . ."

7. Cf. Longacre 1965:125: "Definition of a sentence: a class of syntagmemes of a hierarchical order ranking above such syntagmemes as the clause and below such syntagmemes as the paragraph and discourse. . . . Affirmation, quotation, conditional propositions, balance, antithesis, and chronological or logical sequence (and sometimes question and command) are meanings often expressed by sentence structures." Cf. also Pike and Pike 1982:12–15 (including Display 1.1) for discussion of the sentence as the filler of a tagmeme.

8. These labels are used here since Germanic scholars, with a view toward morphology, often refer to the merged Germanic mood as the optative, and since the (Proto-Indo-European) function corresponding to the optative is Wish.

The following are examples of the merger in Gothic:

(7) (Wish) *Qimai þiudinassus þeins.* "Thy kingdom come" (Matthew 6:10).

(8) (Volition) *(wiljau ei) mis gibais ana mesa haubiþ Iohannis þis daupjandins.* "(I will that) thou give me by and by in a charger the head of John the Baptist" (Mark 6:25). (Cf. Hirt 1934: [III]149.)

The functions of "A:a" and "B:b" have merged between the earlier and the later stage. In terms of the above example of verb phrases, the functions of "Wish:OptSent" and "Volition:SubjSent" have merged, or become noncontrastive, between Proto-Indo-European and Germanic.

2.2.1.2. Syntagmemic. The syntagmemes "A[a]" in 1 and 2 and "B[b]" in 1 and 3 are replaced by "M[a]" in 1, 2, and 3 (cf. fig. 10). In other words, a merger or loss of contrast has taken place between "A[a]" and "B[b]". Such a replacement pattern is found in the merger of the optative clause syntagmeme and the subjunctive clause syntagmeme between Proto-Indo-European and Germanic (see details and references in 2.2.1.1). In other words, PIE "OptCl [. . .]" and "SubjCl [. . .]" are replaced in Germanic by "OptCl [. . .]", where 1 is the contrastive set, 2, characteristic for "OptCl [. . .]", includes OptSent [. . . +Base:___ . . .], and 3, characteristic for "SubCl [. . .]", includes SubjSent [. . . +Base:___ . . .]. The constructional types "A[a]" and "B[b]" have merged between the earlier and later stages. In terms of the above example of clauses, the usages of "OptCl [. . .]" and "SubjCl [. . .]" have merged, or become noncontrastive, between Proto-Indo-European and Germanic.

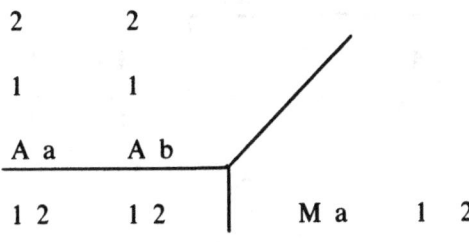

Fig. 11

2.2.1.3. Allotagmatic. The coallotagmas 'A:a' and 'A:b' are replaced by 'M:a' in 1 and 2 (fig. 11). Such a replacement pattern is found among the (inflected) relative pronoun and (uninflected) relative particle allotagmas of the subject tagmeme between Old English (OE) and Middle English (cf. Quirk and Wrenn 1957:72, 98, and Traugott 1972:103f.); thus the Old English allotagmas 'S:RelPn' and 'S:Part' are replaced by ME 'S:RelPn', where 1 is the contrastive set, and 2, characteristic for "S:RelPn/Part...", includes Cl [_ +P: ...]. Since 'M:a' occurs not only where 'A:a' occurred, but also where 'A:b' occurred, this is a tagmemic parallel of the extreme case of analogical change in morphology, where one coallomorph completely invades the territory of another.

2.2.1.4. Allosyntagmatic. The coallosyntagmas 'A[a]' and 'A[b]' are replaced by 'M[a]' in 1 and 2 (cf. fig. 11). Such a replacement pattern is found among the single and double modal allosyntagmas of the verb phrase between Middle English and Standard Modern English (cf. Traugott 1972:115f., 192); thus the Middle English allosyntagmas 'V [+ModAux:modaux +VH:v]' and 'V [+ModAux:modaux +ModAux:modaux +VH:v]' are replaced by the Standard Modern English allotagma 'V [+ModAux:modaux +VH:v]', where 1 is the contrastive set, and 2, characteristic for "V [...]", includes Cl [+S: ... +P_ ...].

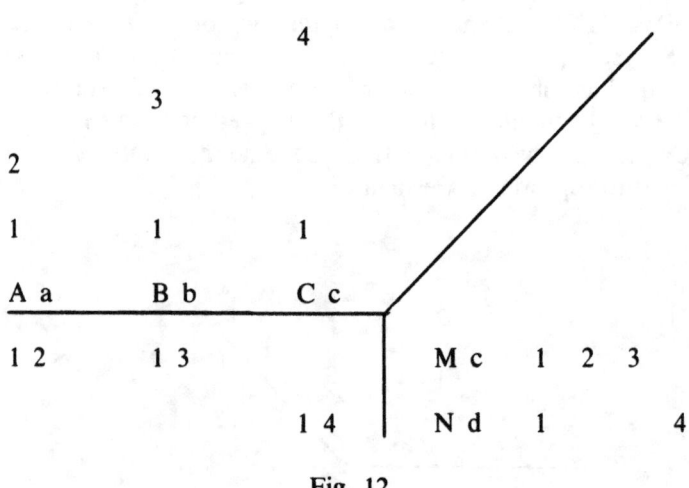

Fig. 12

Tagmemic and Syntagmemic Change

Since 'M[a]' occurs where both 'A[a]' and 'A[b]' occurred, this is a syntagmemic parallel of the extreme case of analogical change in morphology, where one coallomorph completely takes over the territory of another.

2.2.2. Replacement with Semantic Change[9]

2.2.2.1. Tagmemic. Strictly, the replacement pattern discussed in 2.2.1.1 (cf. fig. 10), along with the example accompanying it, is an illustration of emic merger with semantic change as well as an example of regular merger, since the distribution of 'M:a' in 1, 2, and 3 does not match that of 'A:a', namely 1 and 2. Another instance of merger with semantic change occurs when "A:a" in 1 and 2, and "B:b" in 1 and 3 are replaced by "M:c" in 1, 2, and 3, where the allotagma associated with "M:c" was formerly associated with "C:c" of the earlier stage (fig. 12). The provenience of the allotagma of "N:d" is of no concern here. In this subtype of merger, "M:c" is functionally equivalent to "A:a" and "B:b".

Yet another instance of merger with semantic change is syncretism, where the distribution of 'M:a' in 1, 2, and 3 does not match that of 'A:a' in the earlier stage, namely 1 and 2, and where the distribution of 'M:b' in 1, 2, and 3 does not match that of 'B:b' in the earlier stage, namely 1 and 3 (fig. 13).

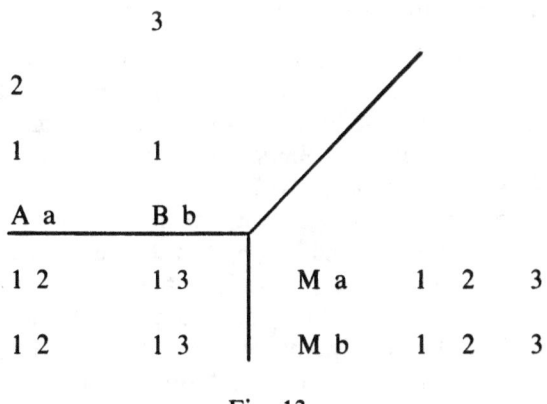

Fig. 13

---

9. Cf. 2.1.2.

Such a replacement pattern is found in the merger of the Volition (subjunctive) tagmeme and the Wish (optative) tagmeme between Proto-Indo-European and Classical Latin (cf. Buck 1933:238, 301 [sect. 425.3] and Prokosch 1939:208). In other words, PIE "Volition:SubjSent" and "Wish:OptSent" are replaced by CL "Volition:$_{(PIE)}$SubjSent/ $_{(PIE)}$OptSent"; cf. 2.2.1.1 for specification of pertinent environments. (As in the case of Germanic, the labels for the merged tagmeme in Classical Latin reflect the terminology of Latin scholars; cf. footnote 8.) See (9)(a) and (b) and (10)(a) and (b) for examples of the merger in Latin:

(9)(a) (Volition [Proto-Indo-European subjunctive]): *(Volo ut) protinus des mihi in disco caput Ioannis Baptistae.* "(I will that) thou give me by and by in a charger the head of John the Baptist" (Mark 6:25).
  (b) (Wish [Proto-Indo-European optative]): *ne vos mortem timueritis* "let ye not fear death" (Lewis 1964:660)
(10)(a) (Wish [Proto-Indo-European subjunctive]): *Adveniat regnum tuum.* "Thy kingdom come" (Matthew 6:10).
  (b) (Wish [Proto-Indo-European optative]): *(velim) verum sit* "(I wish) it may be true" (Lewis 1964:660)

"M:a/b" in 1, 2, and 3 is functionally equivalent to "A:a" and "B:b". Since each of the coallotagmas of "M:a/b" was once associated with contrasting tagmemes, however, this example is also a tagmemic parallel of syncretism in morphology.

2.2.2.2. Syntagmemic. The replacement pattern discussed in 2.2.1.2 (cf. fig. 10), along with the example accompanying it, is not only an illustration of regular merger, but also an illustration of emic merger with semantic change, since the distribution of 'M[a]' in 1, 2, and 3 does not match that of 'A[a]', which is 1 and 2.

A second example of merger with semantic change is observed when "A[a]" in 1 and 2, and "B[b]" in 1 and 3, are replaced by "M[c]" in 1, 2, and 3 where the allosyntagma of "M[c]" formerly belonged to "C[c]" (cf. fig. 12). The source of the allosyntagma of "N[d]" is immaterial at this point. In this subtype of merger, "M[c]" is equivalent as a constructional type to "A[a]" and "B[b]".

A third illustration of merger with semantic change is syncretism, where the distribution of 'M[a]', 1, 2, and 3, does not match that of 'A[a]', namely 1 and 2, and where the distribution of 'M[b]' in 1, 2, and 3 does does not match that of 'B[b]' in the earlier stage, 1 and 3 (cf. fig. 13). Such a replacement pattern is found in the merger of the subjunctive clause syntagmeme and the optative clause syntagmeme between Proto-Indo-European and Classical Latin (cf. Buck 1933:238

and 2.2.2.1). In other words, PIE"SubjCl [... P:SubjV ...]" and "OptCl [... P:OptV ...]" are replaced by CL "SubjCl [... P:(PIE)SubjV / (PIE)OptV ...]", where 1 is the contrastive set, 2, characteristic for "SubjCl [...]", includes SubjSent [+Base:___ ...], and 3, characteristic for "OptCl [...]", includes OptSent [+Base:___ ...]. "M[a/b]" in 1, 2, and 3 is equivalent as a constituent type to "A[a]" and "B[b]". Since the coallosyntagmas of "M[a/b]" were once associated with contrasting syntagmemes, however, this example is also a syntagmemic parallel of syncretism in morphology.

2.2.2.3. Allosyntagmatic. The coallotagmas 'A:a' and 'A:b' are replaced by 'M:c' in 1 and 2 (fig. 14).

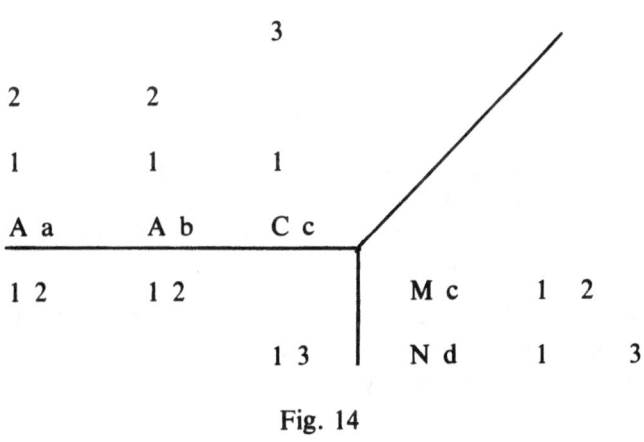

Fig. 14

As in 2.2.2.1 (fig. 12), the merged allotagma of the later stage was formerly associated with another tagmeme, "C:c" in the earlier stage.

2.2.2.4. Allosyntagmatic. The coallosyntagmas 'A[a]' and 'A[b]' are replaced by 'M[c]' in 1 and 2 (cf. fig. 14). As in the case of syntagmemic merger by semantic change (cf. 2.2.2.2 and fig. 12), the merged allosyntagma of the later stage belonged to another syntagmeme, "C[c]", in the earlier stage.

2.2.3. Replacement with Innovation[10]

2.2.3.1. Tagmemic. The tagmemes "A:a" and "B:b" are replaced by "M:c", the allotagma of which has innovation as its source (fig. 15).

10. Cf. 2.1.3.

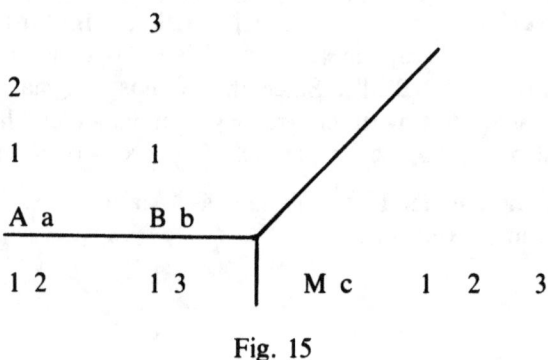

Fig. 15

"M:c" is functionally equivalent to "A:a" and "B:b".

2.2.3.2. Syntagmemic. The syntagmemes "A[a]" and "B[b]" merge, and are replaced by "M[c]", whose allotagma entered the later stage of the language by innovation (cf. fig. 15). Functionally, "M[c]" is equivalent to "A[a]" and "B[b]".

2.2.3.3. Allotagmatic. In this subtype of merger, the coallotagmas 'A:a' and 'A:b' are replaced by the allotagma 'M:c' in 1 and 2; the source of the replacing allotagma is innovation (fig. 16).

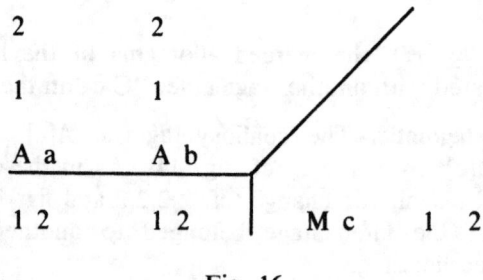

Fig. 16

Such a replacement pattern is found among the perfect and imperfect allotagmas of the passive auxiliary between Middle High German and many varieties of Pennsylvania German (cf. Lockwood 1968:144 and Buffington and Barba 1965:104); thus the Middle High German allotagmas in (11)(a) and (b) are replaced by the Pennsylvania German allotagma in (12)(a), where 1 is the contrastive set and 2, characteristic for "PasAux:pasaux", includes PasV [. . . __ . . . VH:v].

(11)(a) Middle High German perfect: 'PasV [+PasAux:pasaux [+auxnuc:auxst +Conj:conj (=*bin*)] +VH:v]'
  (a') *ich bin gelobet* "I have been praised" (Wright 1955:61)
(b) Middle High German imperfect: 'PasV [+PasAux:pasaux [+auxnuc:auxst +Conj:conj (=*war*)] +VH:v]'
  (b') *ich war gelobet* "I was praised" (Wright 1955:61)

(12)(a) Pennsylvania German perfect: 'PasV [+FinAux:finaux [+auxnuc:auxst +Conj:conj (=*iss*)] +PasAux:pasaux [+auxnuc:auxst (=*warre*)] +VH:v]'
  (a') *er iss genumme warre* "he was/has been taken" (Buffington and Barba 1965:104)

2.2.3.4. Allosyntagmatic. In allosyntagmatic merger with innovation, the coallosyntagmas 'A[a]' and 'A[b]' are replaced by 'A[c]' in 1 and 2; the origin of the allosyntagma of the later stage is innovation (cf. fig. 16). Such a replacement pattern is found among the allosyntagmas of the passive verb phrase between Middle High German and Early Pennsylvania German (cf. [11] [a] and [b], and [12] [a] in 2.2.3.3), where 1 is the contrastive set, and 2, characteristic for "PasV [. . .]", includes PasCl [+S: . . . +P:__ . . .].

2.2.4. Replacement with Borrowing[11]

2.2.4.1. Tagmemic. The replacement pattern of tagmemic merger with borrowing is identical to that of tagmemic merger with innovation as described in 2.2.3.1 (fig. 15). The characteristic of this subtype that differentiates it from other subtypes of merger is that the source of the filler of the replacing tagmeme is borrowing from another language. As in the other subtypes of emic merger, the replacing tagmeme of the late period is functionally equivalent to the tagmemes of the early period that it replaces.

2.2.4.2. Syntagmemic. Syntagmemic merger with borrowing differs only superficially from syntagmemic merger with innovation, described in 2.2.3.2 (fig. 15) in that the source of the allosyntagma of the later

---

11. Cf. 2.1.4.

stage is a foreign language. The replacing syntagmeme is equivalent as a constructional type to the syntagmemes of the earlier stage, which is typical of merger.

2.2.4.3. Allotagmatic. The pattern of allotagmatic merger with borrowing is indicated diagrammatically in figure 16. As in emic merger with borrowing, this subtype differs from other subtypes of merger only in that the source of the allotagma in the later stage is borrowing.

2.2.4.4. Allosyntagmatic. Allosyntagmatic merger with borrowing differs only superficially from allosyntagmatic merger with innovation (cf. 2.2.3.4 and fig. 16). As in emic merger with borrowing, the characteristic of this etic subtype that differentiates it from other subtypes of merger is that the source of the allosyntagma in the later stage is borrowing from another language.

2.3 Split[12]

In emic split, or differentiation, noncontrasting coetic units in an early stage of a language are replaced in all of their environments by contrasting emic units in the later stage; in etic split, an etic member of an emic unit of the earlier stage is replaced in its environments by two or more etic units in the later stage in corresponding environments. Split has three subtypes: regular replacement (which is equivalent, for purposes of reconstruction, to replacement with innovation; cf. the criteria on p. 56 and p. 60), replacement by semantic change, and replacement by borrowing.

Differentiation with replacement by semantic change and borrowing appear at first blush not to be cases of differentiation at all, since, in each of these subtypes, one of the manifesting elements of the later period was obviously not associated with the emic element under discussion at the *earliest* period of the language. However, as the diagram sets in (a) figures 40, 41, 42 and (b) figures 35, 36, 37 show, these manifesting elements did in each case become associated, as coetic elements, with the emic elements in an *intermediate* period of the language, and for this reason it is still appropriate to refer to the linguistic change as differentiation. For the following sections dealing with differentiation, readers may find it helpful to read 3.3.1.1 in conjunction with 2.3.1.1; 3.3.1.2 in conjunction with 2.3.1.2, and so on, even though the approach in chapter 2, as it is reflected in the discussions and diagrams, differs noticeably from that in chapter 3.

---

12. It should be noted here that in split, as opposed to one-to-one replacement and merger, regular replacement overlaps with replacement by innovation; for this reason, there is no section dealing specifically with replacement by innovation.

2.3.1. Regular Replacement[13]

2.3.1.1. Tagmemic. The tagmeme "A:a/b" in 1, 2, and 3 is replaced by "M:a" in 1 and 2, and "N:b" in 1 and 3 (fig. 17).

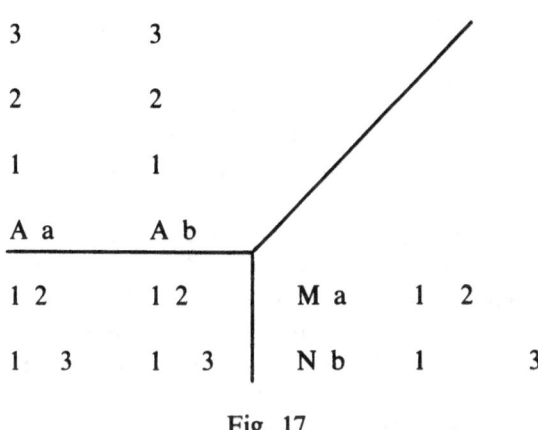

Fig. 17

In other words, "A:a/b" has split by differentiation. Such a replacement pattern is found in the split of the Response tagmeme into the Response tagmeme and the Affirmation tagmeme between Middle and Modern English (cf. Traugott 1972:138ff. and Curme 1947:103).[14] ME "Response:DeclarSent" is replaced by NE "Response:DeclSent" and "Affirm:AffSent", where 1 is the contrastive set, 2, a characteristic set of "Response:DeclarSent" in Middle English and the characteristic set of "Response:DeclarSent" in Modern English, includes Paragraph [. . . +Q:InterrSent[15] +__ . . .], and 3, a characteristic set of

---

13. Cf. 2.1.1.

14. Both Traugott and Curme equate the early construction *do plus infinitive* with the simple form of the verb, and both recognize that this construction eventually took on a particular function. Traugott mentions that "in NE . . . it is the stress, not the *do* that signals the affirmation" (p. 139). Nevertheless, a comparison of (A) with (B), which differ in the presence and absence of *do*, shows that it is *do*, and not the presence or absence of syntactic stress accompanying the finite form of the verb, that correlates with affirmative as opposed to emphatic function.
  (A) (Speaker 1: "You should have *bought* it!") Speaker 2: "I *did* buy it!"—affirmative
  (B) (Speaker 1: "You *stole* it!") Speaker 2: "I *bought* it!"—emphatic

15. Containing a *wh-* word.

"Response:DeclarSent" in Middle English and the characteristic set of "Affirm:AffSent" in Modern English, includes Paragraph [. . . +Command:ImperSent +__ . . .]. This is a tagmemic parallel of differentiation in morphology. The function of "A:a/b" has split by differentiation into the function of "M:a" and the function of "N:b". In terms of the above example of sentence tagmemes in English, the "Response: DeclSent" in Middle English has split into the function of "Response: DeclSent" and the function of "Affirm:AffSent" in Modern English.

2.3.1.2. Syntagmemic. The syntagmeme "A[a/b]" in 1, 2, and 3 is replaced by "M[a]" in 1 and 2, and by "N[b]" in 1 and 3 (cf. fig. 17). That is to say that "A[a/b]" has split by differentiation. Such a replacement pattern is found in the split of the Middle English verb phrase syntagmeme into the (simple) verb phrase syntagmeme and the affirmative verb phrase syntagmeme in Modern English (cf. Traugott 1972:138ff. and Curme 1947:103). ME "V [±FinAux:finaux . . . +VH:v]" is replaced by NE "V [. . . +VH:v]" and "AffV [+AffAux:affaux + VH:v]", where 1 is the contrastive set, 2, a characteristic set of "V [±FinAux:finaux . . . +VH:v]" in Middle English and the characteristic set of "V [. . . +VH:v]" in Modern English, includes Cl [+S: . . . +P:__ . . .], and 3, a characteristic set of "V [±FinAux:finaux . . . +VH:v]" in Middle English and the characteristic set of "AffV [+AffAux:affaux +VH:v]" in Modern English, includes AffCl [+S: . . . +P:__ . . .]. This is a syntagmemic parallel of differentiation in morphology. "A[a/b]" has split by differentiation into "M[a]" and "N[b]". In terms of the above example of English verb phrases, "V [±FinAux:finaux . . . +VH:v]" in Middle English has split into "V [. . . +VH:v]" and "AffV [+AffAux:affaux +VH:v]" in Modern English.

2.3.1.3. Allotagmatic. The allotagma 'A:a' is replaced by the coallotagmas 'M:a' and 'M:b' in 1 and 2 (fig. 18).

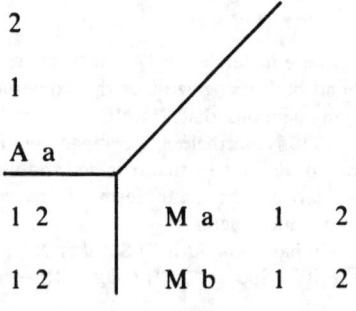

Fig. 18

Such a replacement pattern is found in the split of the genitive allotagma of the possessive tagmeme into the genitive allotagma and the *of*-allotagma between preliterary Old English (OE)[16] and literary Old English. Thus the preliterary Old English allotagma in (13)(a) is replaced by the literary Old English allotagmas in (14)(a) and (14)(b), where 1 is the contrastive set, and 2, characteristic of "Pos: . . .", includes "N [__ . . . +NH:n]".

(13)(a) 'Pos:N [+NH:n [+nnuc:nst +Case:case (= {genitive})]]'

(14)(a) 'Pos:N [+NH:n [+nnuc:nst +Case:case (= {genitive})]]'
   (b) 'Pos:RR [+Relr:prep +Reld:N [+NH:n [nnuc:nst +Case:case (= {dative})]]]'

2.3.1.4. Allosyntagmatic. The allosyntagma 'A[a]' is replaced by 'M[a]' and 'M[b]' in 1 and 2 (cf. fig. 18). Such a replacement pattern is found in the split of the simple allosyntagma of the verb phrase into the simple and the complex allosyntagmas of the verb phrase between Old and Middle English (cf. Traugott 1972:138). OE 'V [+VH:v]' is replaced by ME 'V [+VH:v]' and 'V [+FinAux:finaux +VH:v]', where 1 is the contrastive set, and 2, characteristic for "V [. . .]", includes Cl [+S: . . . +P:__ . . .].

2.3.2. Replacement by Semantic Change[17]

2.3.2.1. Tagmemic. Strictly, the replacement pattern discussed in 2.3.1.1 (cf. fig. 17), and the example accompanying it, is an illustration of emic differentiation with semantic change as well as an example of differentiation by regular replacement, since the distribution of 'M:a', 1 and 2, does not match that of 'A:a', namely 1, 2, and 3. (Likewise, the distribution of 'N:b' does not match that of 'A:b'.) Another instance of differentiation with semantic change occurs when "A:a" in 1, 2, and 3 is replaced by "M:a" in 1 and 2, and "N:c" in 1 and 3, where the allotagma associated with "N:c" was formerly associated with "C:c" (fig. 19). The provenience of the allotagma of "O:d" is of no concern here. In this subtype of differentiation, "M:a" and "N:c" are functionally equivalent to "A:a". Since the filler of "N:c" was associated with "C:c" in the earlier stage, this is another tagmemic parallel of differentiation with semantic change in morphology.

16. This stage of preliterary Old English was implied by Curme (1931:74) when he wrote, "Although in oldest English, the simple genitive was the usual form, the *new* [italics mine—JC] prepositional genitive was in certain categories coming into use by reason of the strong concrete force of *of*, originally meaning *from*, which indicated more graphically the ideas of separation, source, and origin than the simple genitive."

17. Cf. 2.1.2.

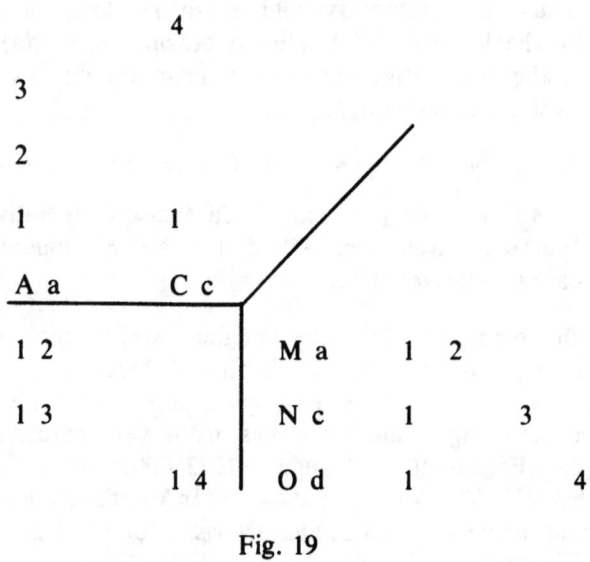

Fig. 19

2.3.2.2. Syntagmemic. The replacement pattern discussed in 2.3.1.2 (cf. fig. 17) together with the example accompanying it, is not only an illustration of differentiation by regular replacement, but also one of differentiation with semantic change, since the distribution of 'M[a]' in 1 and 2 does not match that of 'A[a]', namely 1, 2, and 3 (and the distribution of 'N[b]' does not match that of 'A[b]'). A second illustration of split with semantic change is when "A[a]" in 1, 2, and 3 is replaced by "M[a]" in 1 and 2, and "N[c]" in 1 and 3, where the allosyntagma belonging to "N[c]" belonged to "C[c]" in the earlier stage (cf. fig. 19). The source of the allosyntagma of "O[d]" is immaterial for this example. "M[a]" and "N[c]" as contrastive emic units are equivalent to "A[a]". Because the allosyntagma of "N[c]" formerly belonged to "C[c]", this is another syntagmemic parallel of differentiation with semantic change in morphology.

2.3.2.3. Allotagmatic. The allotagma 'A:a' in 1 and 2 is replaced by 'M:a' and 'M:b' in 1 and 2 (and 'B:a' and 'B:b' in 1 and 3 are replaced by 'N:a' and 'N:b', respectively, in 1 and 3)(fig. 20). Such a pattern is found in the replacement of the genitive allotagma and the prepositional—i.e., the relater-related (Pike and Pike 1982:28)—allotagma (the

Tagmemic and Syntagmemic Change

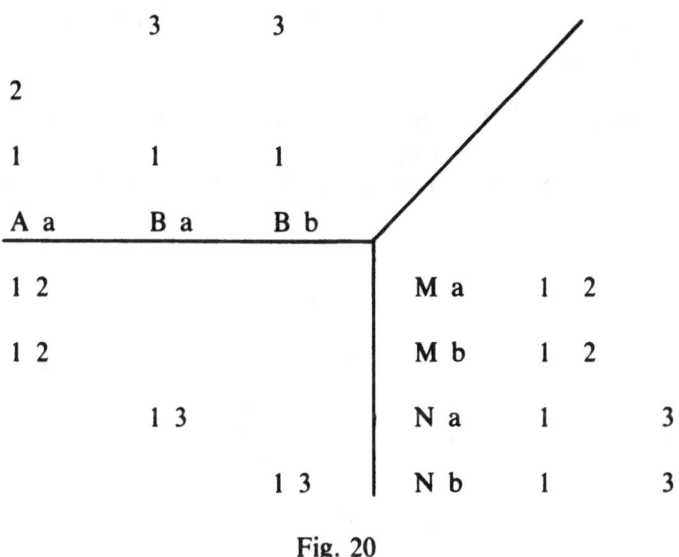

Fig. 20

latter of which formerly belonged to the Noun-Adverbial tagmeme)[18] in the Possession tagmeme between Early Old English and Late Old English/Early Middle English (cf. Traugott 1972:77, 123). Thus, in the earlier stage, the Possession tagmeme had the allotagma in (15)(a), and the Noun-Adverbial tagmeme had the allotagmas in (16)(a) and (b); in the later stage, however, the Possession tagmeme had the allotagmas in (15)(a) and (b), and the Noun-Adverbial tagmeme retained the allotagmas in (16)(a) and (b) of the earlier stage.

(15)(a) Pos:N [+NH:n [+nnuc:nst +Case:case]]
  (a') þa cinges þegnas "the king's thanes" (Quirk and Wrenn 1957:76)
  (b) Pos:RR [+Relr:prep +Reld:N [±Det:det +NH:n [+nnuc:nst +Case:case]]]
  (b') *Here in the temple of the goddesse Clemence* "Here in the temple of the goddess Clemency" (Hopper 1949:59 [Chaucer, *The Knight's Tale*, line 70])

(16)(a) NAdv:N [+NH:n [+nnuc:nst +Case:case]]
  (a') *Beowulf Geata* "Beowulf of the Geats" (Quirk and Wrenn 1957:62)

---

18. The semantic role of the Noun-Adverbial tagmeme in this section is Origin.

(b) NAdv:RR [+Relr:prep +Reld:N [±Det:det +NH:n [+nnuc: nst +Case:case]]]

(b') þa men of Lundenbyrig "the men of London" (Bright 1935:23)

Another instance of etic split with semantic change occurs when the allotagma 'A:a' is replaced by 'M:a' and 'M:b' in 1 and 2, where the second filler of "M:a/b" was formerly the filler of "B:b" (fig. 21).

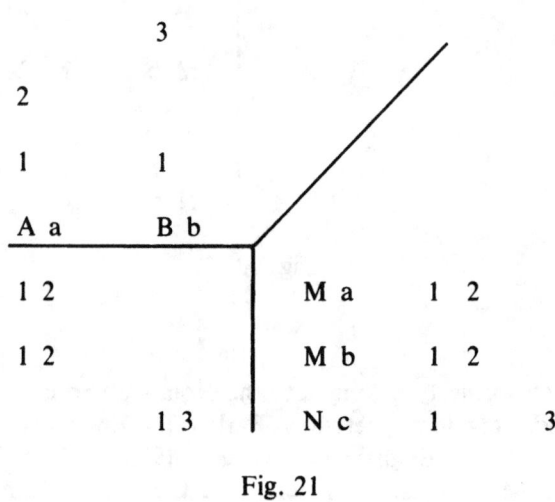

Fig. 21

The origin of the filler of "N:c" is of no concern here.

2.3.2.4. Allosyntagmatic. The allosyntagma 'A[a]' in 1 and 2 is replaced by 'M[a]' and 'M[b]' in 1 and 2 (and 'B[a]' and 'B[b]' in 1 and 3 are replaced by 'N[a]' and 'N[b]', respectively, in 1 and 3)(cf. fig. 20). A second instance of allosyntagmatic split with semantic change is when the allosyntagma 'A[a]' is replaced by 'M[a]' and 'M[b]' in 1 and 2, and where the allosyntagma of "M[b]" belonged to "B[b]" in the earlier stage (fig. 21). The provenience of 'N(c)' is of no concern in this example.

2.3.3. Replacement with Borrowing[19]

2.3.3.1. Tagmemic. "A:a" in 1, 2, and 3 is replaced by "M:a" in 1 and 2, and "N:b" in 1 and 3 (fig. 22).

19. Cf. 2.1.4.

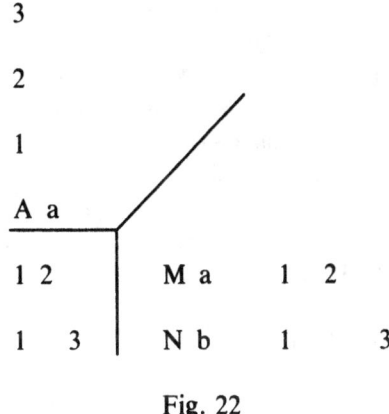

Fig. 22

"A:a" has split by differentiation, and the allotagma associated with "N:b" is borrowed from another language. The function of "A:a" has split into the function of "M:a" and the function of "N:b". It is only from the point of view of manifestation mode that one may distinguish this subtype from other subtypes of differentiation.

2.3.3.2. Syntagmemic. "A[a]" in 1, 2, and 3 is replaced by "M[a]" in 1 and 2, and "N[b]" in 1 and 3 (fig. 22). "A[a]" has split by differentiation, and the allosyntagma belonging to "N[b]" has been taken into the later stage from a foreign language. The function of "A[a]" as an emic unit has split into the contrastive emic units "M[a]" and "N[b]".

2.3.3.3. Allotagmatic. The allotagma 'A:a' is replaced by 'M:a' and 'M:b' in 1 and 2 (fig. 23).

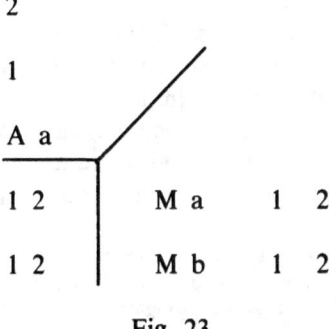

Fig. 23

The second allotagma of 'M:a/b' is not associated with any tagmeme in the earlier stage; instead, it is borrowed from a foreign language. Such a replacement pattern is found in the allotagmas of the passive auxiliary tagmeme between early Pennsylvania German and a recent variety of Pennsylvania German, Southeastern Pennsylvania German SPG). The older Pennsylvania German allotagma in (17)(a) is replaced by the Southeastern Pennsylvania German allotagmas in (17)(a) and (b)—the latter of which is borrowed from English (cf. Costello 1978b)—where 1 is the contrastive set and 2, characteristic for "PasAux:pasaux", includes PasV [. . . ___ . . . +VH:v].

(17)(a) 'PasV [+FinAux:finaux [+auxnuc:auxst +Conj:conj (=*sin*)] +PasAux:pasaux [+auxnuc:auxst (=*warre*)] +VH:v]'
   (a') *Die Gleeder sin vun sellre Fraa gmacht warre.* "The clothes were/have been made by that woman" (Buffington and Barba 1965:105).
  (b) 'PasV [+PasAux:pasaux [+auxnuc:auxst +Conj:conj (= *waar*)] +VH:v]'
   (b') *Der Pitscher waar verbroche bei der Anna.* "The pitcher was broken by Anna" (Costello 1978b:32).

2.3.3.4. Allosyntagmatic. The allosyntagma 'A[a]' is replaced by 'M[a]' and 'M[b]' in 1 and 2 (cf. fig. 23). The second allosyntagma of "M[a/b]" is not the descendant of any syntagmeme in the earlier stage; rather it is a borrowing from another language. Such a replacement pattern is found in the passive verb phrase between early Pennsylvania German and Southeastern Pennsylvania German. Cf. 2.3.3.3, where the older Pennsylvania German allosyntagma in (17)(a) is replaced by the Southeastern Pennsylvania German allosyntagmas in (17)(a) and (b), where 1 is the contrastive set, and 2, characteristic for "PasV [. . .]", includes PasCl [+S: . . . +P:___ . . .].

2.4 Amorphous Loss or Disappearance

In amorphous loss considered from an emic point of view, a tagmeme and ∅[20] are replaced in each of their environments in the earlier stage by ∅ in the later stage. In amorphous loss viewed from the perspective of etic units, the allotagma(s) manifesting a tagmeme, and ∅, are replaced in each of their environments in the earlier stage by ∅ in the later stage (cf. note 3 of this chapter, and the last sentence

---

20. One may paraphrase a statement of Hoenigswald's (1960:35) concerning ∅ in morphological change in order to understand better its role in tagmemic change: Synchronically, ∅ denotes the absence of tagmemes, with the proviso that it is said to occur (in fact, any number of ∅'s are said to occur) as part of any occurring construct.

in 2.4.2). Thus amorphous loss constitutes a special case of merger with ∅.

2.4.1. Tagmemic. The tagmeme "A:a" and ∅ in 1 and 2 are replaced by ∅ in 1 and 2 (fig. 24).

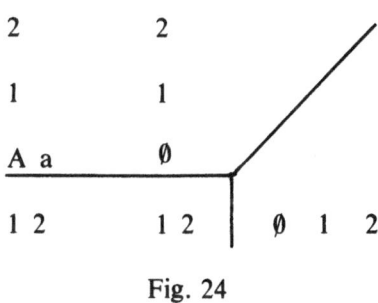

Fig. 24

Thus, "A:a" is lost amorphously. Such a replacement pattern is found in the loss of the interrogative tagmeme between Latin and Romance. In other words, Latin "Int:int" (manifested at morpheme level as the enclitic -*ne*) merges with ∅ in Romance, where 1 is the contrastive set, and 2, the characteristic set, includes V [+VH:v__] (cf. Hoenigswald 1960:35, 4.2.3). The syntactic function of "A:a" has merged with that of ∅ to become ∅; that is to say, the syntactic function of "A:a" has disappeared. In terms of the above illustration, the syntactic function of "Int:int" has disappeared between Latin and Romance.

2.4.2. Allotagmatic. The allotagma 'A:a' and ∅ in 1 and 2 are replaced by ∅ in 1 and 2; in other words, 'A:a' is lost amorphously (cf. fig. 24). The example in 2.4.1 of the merger of Latin "Int:int" with ∅ may also serve as an example of etic merger with ∅. It is worthy of note that etic merger with ∅ occurs only with emic merger with ∅. Cases in which a tagmeme is replaced between the earlier and later stages, and where the number of coallotagmas is lower in the later stage than in the earlier one, are viewed as instances of etic merger (cf. 2.2.1.3, 2.2.2.3, 2.2.3.3, and 2.2.4.3).

2.5 Amorphous Gain or Increment

In amorphous gain, ∅ in a number of environments in the earlier stage is replaced by an emic unit and ∅ in corresponding environments in the later stage; likewise, ∅ in a number of environments in the earlier stage may be replaced by an etic member of an emic unit and ∅ in corresponding environments in the later stage (cf. the last sentence in 2.5.2). These then are special instances of the split of ∅.

2.5.1. Tagmemic. ∅ in 1 and 2 is replaced by "A:a" and ∅ in 1 and 2 (fig. 25).

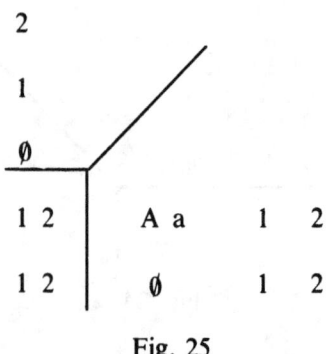

Fig. 25

In other words, "A:a" appears amorphously. Such a replacement pattern is found in the emergence of the modal auxiliary tagmeme between Proto-Indo-European and Germanic (cf. Prokosch 1939:187–93, Curme 1931:393f.). Thus, ∅ is (partially) replaced by "ModAux: modaux" in Germanic, where 1 is the contrastive set, and 2, a characteristic set, includes V [. . . ___ . . . +VH:v]. In tagmemic increment, the syntactic function of "A:a" appears amorphously in the later stage. In terms of this illustration, the syntactic function of "ModAux: modaux" emerges in Germanic.

2.5.2. Allotagmatic. ∅ is replaced by 'A:a' and ∅ in 1 and 2; that is to say, 'A:a' appears amorphously (cf. fig. 25). The above example of the emergence of the modal auxiliary from ∅ may also serve as an example of etic emergence from ∅. It should be mentioned that etic emergence from ∅ occurs only with emic emergence from ∅. Instances in which a tagmeme occurring in the earlier stage is replaced in the later stage, and where the number of coallotagmas is higher in the later stage than in the earlier one, are viewed as cases of etic split (cf. 2.3.1.3, 2.3.2.3, and 2.3.3.3).

3 Tagmemic, Syntagmemic, Allotagmatic, and Allosyntagmatic Reconstruction

In this chapter the principles of the comparative method (1.4) and criteria of internal and comparative reconstruction will be applied to the major types of replacement patterns that affect tagmemes, syntagmemes, allotagmas, and allosyntagmas; these include one-to-one replacement, merger, split (and the subtypes of these patterns, namely, regular replacement, replacement by semantic change, replacement by innovation, and replacement by borrowing), amorphous loss, and amorphous gain.

3.1 One-to-one Replacement

3.1.1. Regular Replacement

3.1.1.1. Tagmemic. In this subtype, neither language changes tagmemically, so that the following correspondences are observed:

L_1	L_2		
"M:a"	"T:a"	1/1	2/2
"N:b"	"U:b"	1/1	3/3

Following the first principle expressed in 1.4 (see p. 10), repeated in abbreviated form here for convenience,

(1) Sets of correspondences of tagmemes and syntagmemes between two daughter languages may be considered to be continuations of respective prototagmemes and protosyntagmemes in the parent language,

we may obtain the reconstruction expressed diagrammatically in figure 26.

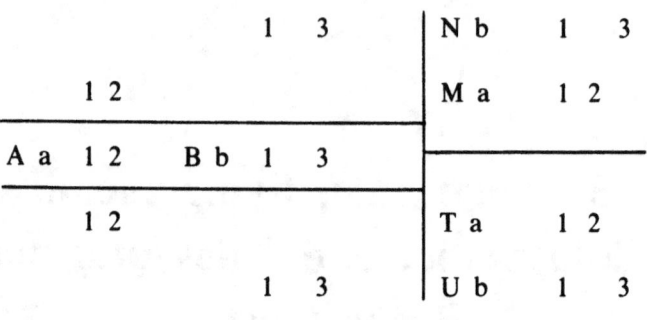

Fig. 26

For example, "Modf:adj" and "NH:n" in New High German and Pennsylvania German lead us to posit these tagmemes in the common ancestor of these languages, Early New High German. (This reconstruction, and those of all other examples in this chapter, except of course those referring to protolanguages, are confirmed by attestations.)

3.1.1.2. Syntagmemic. In this subtype, if neither language changes syntagmemically, the following correspondences may be observed:

L_1	L_2			
"M[a]"	"T[a]"	1/1	2/2	
"N[b]"	"U[b]"	1/1		3/3

Following the principle in (1), a reconstruction is obtained (cf. fig. 26). For example, the kernel syntagmeme TrCl [+S:N +P:TrV [+VH:trv] +O:N] and the derived syntagmeme PasTrCl [+S:N +P:TrV [PasAux: pasaux +VH:trv] +PAdv:RR] in Spanish and French enable us to posit these syntagmemes in their common ancestor, Vulgar Latin (cf. Muller and Taylor 1932:68, 235; also 63, 206 for examples from the second half of the eighth century). It should be noted here that if one posits for the protolanguage several syntagmemes (or allosyntagmas) that are linked by a transformation in each of the daughter languages, then one should posit that transformation for the protolanguage also. Thus, in the above case, one would reconstruct for Vulgar Latin not only active kernel and passive derived syntagmemes, but also the passive transformation that captures the relationship that exists between them in the daughter languages and the protolanguage. Cf. Costello (1975) and Melchart (1981) for other proposals to reconstruct transformations.

Allosyntagmatic Reconstruction

3.1.1.3. Allotagmatic. In this subtype, if neither language changes allotagmatically, the following correspondence is observed:

L_1 L_2
'M:a/b'   'T:a/b'   1/1   2/2

Following both the first principle (p. 39) and also the second principle expressed in 1.4 (see p. 11), repeated here for convenience,

(2) No etic characteristics of emic units aside from those that are distributed in each of the daughter languages involved in a reconstruction should be assigned to the protoemic units of the parent language,

a set like the one above will yield a reconstruction (cf. fig. 27).

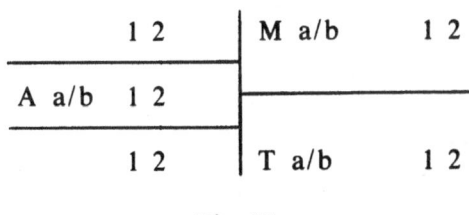

Fig. 27

For example, 'S:N' and 'S:Pn' in Spanish and French yield these allotagmas in the common ancestor of these languages, Vulgar Latin.

3.1.1.4. Allosyntagmatic. In this subtype, the following correspondence results when neither language changes allosyntagmatically:

L_1 L_2
'M[a/b]'   'T[a/b]'   1/1   2/2

Following (1) and (2), a set like the one above will yield the reconstruction in figure 27. For example, 'N [+Det:det +NH:n]' and 'N [+Det:det +NH:n +Modf:adj]' in Spanish and French enable us to reconstruct these allotagmas in the common ancestor of these languages, Vulgar Latin.

3.1.2. Replacement with Semantic Change

3.1.2.1. Tagmemic. If the semantic change in L_1 is not duplicated in L_2, a reconstruction of functions is possible, but according to the second principle, a reconstruction of fillers is not. For example, from the correspondence sets

L_1	L_2			
"M:[b]"	"T:[a]"	1/1	2/2	
"N:[c]"	"U:[b]"	1/1		3/3

a reconstruction is limited to one of functions only, as in figure 28. (In this replacement pattern subtype, and in all the following, if the change in L_1 is duplicated in L_2, then the change is irretrievable, and what results in each instance is a case that appears to be equivalent to one-to-one regular replacement.)

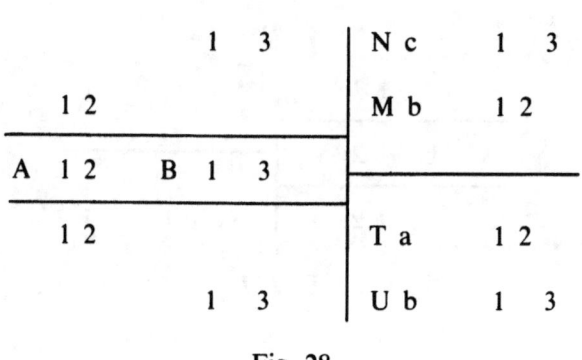

Fig. 28

3.1.2.2. Syntagmemic. If the semantic change occurs in L_1 only, a reconstruction of syntagmemes as emically contrasting units is possible, but according to the principle in (2) (p. 41), a reconstruction of the allosyntagmas (or constituents) is not. For the correspondence sets a reconstruction is limited to the one represented diagrammatically in figure 28.

L_1	L_2			
"M[b]"	"T[a]"	1/1	2/2	
"N[c]"	"U[b]"	1/1		3/3

3.1.2.3 Allotagmatic. If the semantic change is limited to L_1, as in the following,

Allosyntagmatic Reconstruction

L_1	L_2			
'M:b'	'T:a'	1/1	2/2	
'N:c'	'U:b'	1/1		3/3

then according to the second principle, a reconstruction of the protoallotagmas is not possible (cf. fig. 28).

3.1.2.4. Allosyntagmatic. If there is a semantic change in L_1, but not in L_2, as follows,

L_1	L_2			
'M[b]'	'T[a]'	1/1	2/2	
'N[c]'	'U[b]'	1/1		3/3

then according to the second principle, one cannot reconstruct the appropriate protoallosyntagmas (cf. fig. 28).

3.1.3. Replacement with Innovation

3.1.3.1. Tagmemic. If the innovative change occurs in L_1 only, as in the following,

L_1	L_2			
"M:c"	"T:a"	1/1	2/2	
"N:b"	"U:b"	1/1		3/3

then according to the principle in (2), a reconstruction of the filler of "A", the prototagmeme that was affected by the innovative replacement, is not possible, although the function is reconstructible. ("B:b" on the other hand is fully reconstructible.) Cf. figure 29.

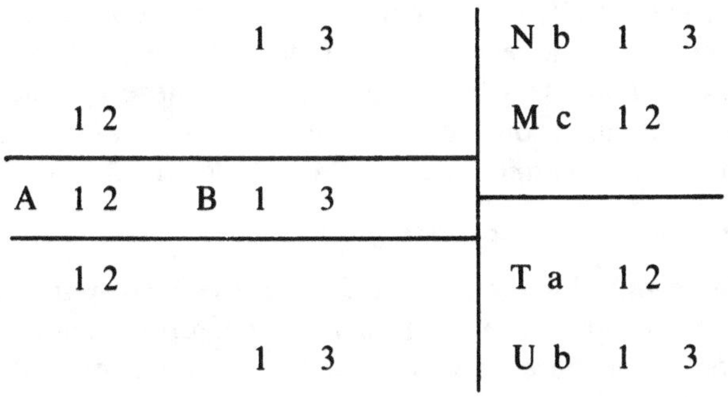

Fig. 29

3.1.3.2. Syntagmemic. If the innovative change in L_1 is not duplicated in L_2, as in the following,

L_1	L_2		
"M[c]"	"T[a]"	1/1	2/2
"N[b]"	"U[b]"	1/1	3/3

a reconstruction of the allosyntagma of "A", the protosyntagmeme that was affected by the innovative replacement, is not possible, according to (2), although the syntagmeme as a contrasting emic unit is reconstructible. ("B[b]", on the other hand, is fully reconstructible.) Cf. figure 29.

3.1.3.3. Allotagmatic. If there is an innovative change in L_1 but not in L_2, as in

L_1	L_2		
'M:c'	'T:a'	1/1	2/2
'N:b'	'U:b'	1/1	3/3

then according to (2), one cannot reconstruct the protoallotagma of "A". Cf. figure 29.

3.1.3.4. Allosyntagmatic. If the innovative change is limited to L_1, as in

L_1	L_2		
'M[c]'	'T[a]'	1/1	2/2
'N[b]'	'U[b]'	1/1	3/3

then according to the principle in (2), a reconstruction of the protoallosyntagma of "A" is not possible (cf. fig. 29). For example, 'PasTrV [+PasAux:pasaux +VH:v]', the present tense allosyntagma of the transitive passive verb phrase in Vulgar Latin, and 'PasTrV [+VH: pasv]', the present tense allosyntagma of the transitive passive verb phrase in Late Greek, would not enable us to reconstruct the allosyntagma at the phrase level for Proto-Indo-European. Moreover, it goes without saying that even the oldest stages of these daughter languages do not enable us to reconstruct the *morphs* of the passive (middle) conjugation at the morphemic level for Proto-Indo-European.

3.1.4. Replacement with Borrowing

3.1.4.1. Tagmemic. In this type of change, the correspondence sets will be identical to those in 3.1.3.1, one-to-one replacement with innovation, except that here the source of the filler of "M:c" will be

Allosyntagmatic Reconstruction

borrowing rather than innovation; the limitations on reconstruction will be the same as those in 3.1.3.1.

3.1.4.2. Syntagmemic. The correspondence sets in this type of change will be identical to those in 3.1.3.2, syntagmemic one-to-one replacement with innovation, with the exception that the source of the allosyntagma of "M[c]" will be borrowing, not innovation; the limits on reconstruction in 3.1.3.2 will hold here also.

3.1.4.3. Allotagmatic. In this type of change, the correspondence sets that result will be the same as those in 3.1.3.3, allotagmatic one-to-one replacement with innovation, except that 'M:c' will originate in borrowing rather than innovation; the reconstructional limitations will be identical to those in 3.1.3.3. For example, 'PasAux:pasaux$_{(foreign)}$ [+auxnuc:auxst$_{(calque)}$ + Conj:conj]', the Southeastern Pennsylvania German present passive auxiliary allotagma borrowed from English, and 'PasAux:pasaux$_{(native)}$ [+auxnuc:auxst +Conj:conj]', the native Modern Standard German present passive auxiliary allotagma, would not enable us to reconstruct the allotagma for Early New High German.

3.1.4.4 Allosyntagmatic. The correspondence sets resulting from this type of change will be identical to those in 3.1.3.4, allosyntagmatic one-to-one replacement with innovation, the only exception being that the source of 'M[c]' will be borrowing, not innovation; the limitations on reconstruction in 3.1.3.4 will be the same here. For example, 'PasTrV [+PasAux:pasaux$_{(foreign)}$ +VH:v]', the Southeastern Pennsylvania German present passive allosyntagma borrowed from English, and 'PasTrV [+PasAux:pasaux$_{(native)}$ +VH:v]', the native Modern Standard German present passive allosyntagma, would not lead us to reconstruct the allosyntagma for Early New High German.

	1 2		1 3	M a	1 2 3
A a	1 2	B	1 3		
	1 2			T a	1 2
			1 3	U b	1 3

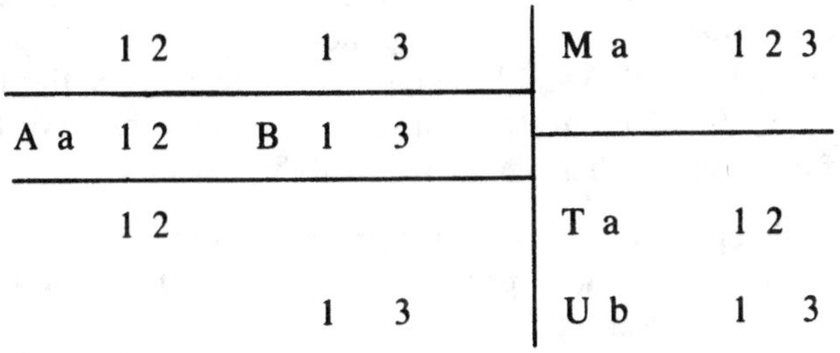

Fig. 30

3.2 Merger

3.2.1. Regular Replacement

3.2.1.1. Tagmemic. If the merger in L_1 is not duplicated in L_2, as in the following,

L_1	L_2		
"M:a"	"T:a"	1/1	2/2
"M:a"	"U:b"	1/1	3/3

a reconstruction of the function of "B", the prototagmeme that was affected by the merger, is possible, but according to (2), a reconstruction of fillers is not. ("A:a", on the other hand, is fully reconstructible.) Cf. figure 30. For example, Germanic "Wish:OptSent" corresponding to Greek "Wish:OptSent" ("Der Optativ steht als Wunschmodus . . ." Hirt 1934:[III] 149) and to "Volition:SubjSent" ("Der Konjunktiv steht als Adhortativus oder Volitivus." Hirt 1934:[III] 145) would lead us to reconstruct the function and filler for one tagmeme, "Wish:OptSent", but only the function for the other tagmeme.

3.2.1.2. Syntagmemic. If the merger occurs in L_1 only, as in the following,

L_1	L_2		
"M[a]"	"T[a]"	1/1	2/2
"M[a]"	"U[b]"	1/1	3/3

a reconstruction of "B", the protosyntagmeme that was affected by the merger, as an emically contrasting unit, is possible, but according to (2), a reconstruction of the allotagmas (or constituents) is not. ("A[a]" on the other hand is fully reconstructible.) Cf. figure 30. For example, Germanic "OptCl [. . .]" corresponding to Greek "OptCl [. . .]" and "SubjCl [. . .]" would enable us to reconstruct the two syntagmemes as contrasting constructions, but we could retrieve the allosyntagma of only one of them, namely "OptCl [. . .]".

3.2.1.3. Allotagmatic. If the merger is limited to L_1 (i.e., the replacement of two or more protoallotagmas by one of these allotagmas in L_1), as in the following,

L_1	L_2		
'M:a'	'T:a/b'	1/1	2/2

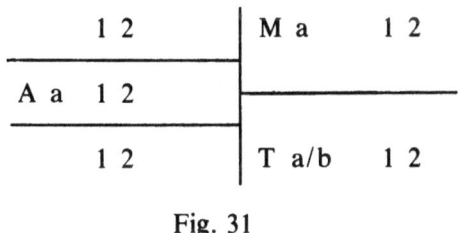

Fig. 31

then according to the principle in (2), a reconstruction of only one protoallotagma of "A" is possible, and thus the desired reconstruction is not achieved (cf. fig. 31). For example, ME 'S:RelPn' corresponding to Old Frisian (OF) 'S:RelPn' and 'S:Part' (Steller 1928:56) would lead us to reconstruct only the allotagma 'S:RelPn' for Proto-Anglo-Frisian, which, according to Prokosch (1939:277), is incorrect.

3.2.1.4. Allosyntagmatic. If there is a merger in L_1 (i.e., the replacement of two or more protoallosyntagmas by one of the allosyntagmas in L_1), but not in L_2, as in the following,

L_1 L_2
'M[a]'   'T[a/b]'   1/1   2/2

then according to (2), one can reconstruct only one protoallosyntagma of "A"; thus the desired reconstruction is not achieved (cf. fig. 31). For example, Standard NE 'V [+ModAux:modaux +VH:v]' corresponding to Southern Nonstandard English 'V [+ModAux:modaux +VH:v]' and 'V [+ModAux:modaux +ModAux:modaux +VH:v]' (cf. Traugott 1972:192) would enable us to reconstruct only the allosyntagma 'V [+ModAux:modaux +VH:v]' for Middle English.

```
           1 2       1 3    | M c     1 2 3
       A 1 2    B 1 3       |
           1 2              | T a     1 2
                    1 3     | U b     1 3
```

Fig. 32

3.2.2. Replacement with Semantic Change

3.2.2.1. Tagmemic. If the merger with semantic change occurs in L_1 only (where the protoallotagmas of two prototagmemes are replaced in a merged tagmeme by the protoallotagma of a third prototagmeme), as in the following,

L_1	L_2		
"M:c"	"T:a"	1/1	2/2
"M:c"	"U:b"	1/1	3/3

then because of the principle stated in (2), a reconstruction of the fillers of "A" and "B" is not possible, although the functions are reconstructible (cf. fig. 32). (Cf. 3.2.1.1, which technically is also a case of tagmemic merger with semantic change [and where the allotagmas merge].)

If the merger with semantic change occurs in L_1 only (where each of the protoallotagmas of two prototagmemes appears in the replacing merged tagmeme [i.e., syncretism]), as in the following,

L_1	L_2		
"M:a/b"	"T:a"	1/1	2/2
"M:a/b"	"U:b"	1/1	3/3

then because of the principle stated in (2), one may reconstruct the correct fillers of "A" and "B" (cf. fig. 33).

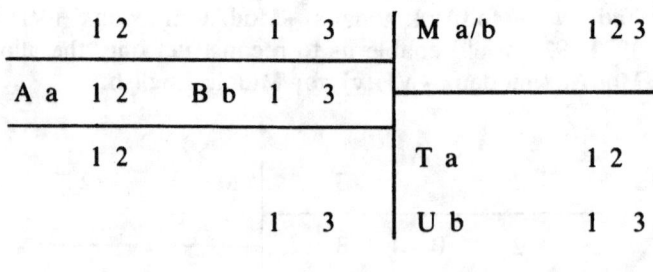

Fig. 33

For example, Latin "Volition:$_{(PIE)}$SubjSent/$_{(PIE)}$OptSent" corresponding to Greek "Volition:SubjSent" and "Wish:OptSent" would lead one to reconstruct the correct fillers of each of the two tagmemes in Proto-Indo-European.

3.2.2.2. Syntagmemic.

If the merger with semantic change in L_1 (where the protoallosyntagmas of two protosyntagmemes are replaced in a merged tagmeme by the protoallosyntagma of a third protosyntagmeme) is not duplicated in L_2, as in the following,

L_1	L_2		
"M[c]"	"T[a]"	1/1	2/2
"M[c]"	"U[b]"	1/1	3/3

a reconstruction of "A" and "B" as emically contrasting units is possible, but according to (2), a reconstruction of the allosyntagmas (or constituents) is not; cf. figure 32. (Cf. 3.2.1.2, which technically is also a case of syntagmemic merger by semantic change where the allosyntagmas merge.)

If the merger with semantic change in L_1 (where each of the protoallosyntagmas of two protosyntagmemes appears in the replacing merged syntagmeme [i.e., syncretism]) is not duplicated in L_2, as in the following,

L_1	L_2		
"M[a/b]"	"T[a]"	1/1	2/2
"M[a/b]"	"U[b]"	1/1	3/3

then because of the principle stated in (2), one may reconstruct the correct allosyntagmas of "A" and "B"; cf. figure 33. For example, Latin "SubjCl [. . . +P:$_{(PIE)}$SubjV/$_{(PIE)}$OptV . . .]" corresponding to Greek "SubjCl [. . . +P:SubjV . . .]" and "OptCl [. . . +P:OptV . . .]" would enable us to reconstruct the correct allosyntagmas of each of the two syntagmemes in Proto-Indo-European.

3.2.2.3. Allotagmatic.

If there is a merger with semantic change in L_1, where the protoallotagmas of one prototagmeme are replaced in the later stage by the protoallotagma of a second prototagmeme, but not in L_2, as in figure 34,

L_1	L_2		
M c	T a/b	1/1	2/2

Fig. 34

then considering the principle stated in (2), it is impossible to reconstruct any protoallotagma.

3.2.2.4. Allosyntagmatic. If the merger with semantic change is limited to L_1, where the protoallosyntagmas of one protosyntagmeme are replaced in the later stage by the protoallosyntagma of a second protosyntagmeme, as in figure 34, then according to the principle stated in (2), it is impossible to reconstruct any protoallosyntagma.

3.2.3. Replacement with Innovation

3.2.3.1. Tagmemic. If the merger with innovation in L_1 is not duplicated in L_2, as in the following,

L_1	L_2			
"M:c"	"T:a"	1/1	2/2	
"M:c"	"U:b"	1/1		3/3

a reconstruction of the functions of "A" and "B" is possible, but according to the principle in (2), a reconstruction of the fillers is not (cf. fig. 32).

3.2.3.2. Syntagmemic. If the merger with innovation occurs in L_1, as in the following,

L_1	L_2			
"M[c]"	"T[a]"	1/1	2/2	
"M[c]"	"U[b]"	1/1		3/3

a reconstruction of the syntagmemes as contrasting emic units is possible, but according to the principle in (2), a reconstruction of the allosyntagmas (or constituents) is not (cf. fig. 32).

3.2.3.3. Allotagmatic. If the merger with innovation is limited to L_1, as in figure 34, then according to the principle in (2), it is impossible to reconstruct any protoallotagmas.

3.2.3.4. Allosyntagmatic. If there is a merger with innovation in L_1, but not in L_2, as in figure 34, then according to (2), it is impossible to reconstruct any protoallosyntagmas.

3.2.4. Replacement with Borrowing

3.2.4.1. Tagmemic. If the merger with borrowing occurs in L_1 only, as in the following,

L_1	L_2			
"M:c"	"T:a"	1/1	2/2	
"M:c"	"U:b"	1/1		3/3

Allosyntagmatic Reconstruction

a reconstruction of the functions of "A" and "B" is possible, but according to (2), a reconstruction of the fillers in not (cf. fig. 32).

3.2.4.2. Syntagmemic. If the merger with borrowing in L_1 is not duplicated in L_2, as in the following,

L_1	L_2		
"M[c]"	"T[a]"	1/1	2/2
"M[c]"	"U[b]"	1/1	3/3

a reconstruction of the syntagmemes as contrasting emic units is possible, but according to the principle in (2), a reconstruction of the allosyntagmas in not (cf. fig. 32).

3.2.4.3. Allotagmatic. If there is a merger with borrowing in L_1, but not in L_2, as in figure 34, then according to (2), it is impossible to reconstruct any protoallotagmas.

3.2.4.4. Allosyntagmatic. If the merger with borrowing is limited to L_1, as in figure 34, then according to (2), it is impossible to reconstruct any protoallosyntagmas.

3.3 Split

3.3.1. Regular Replacement

3.3.1.1. Tagmemic. If the split by differentiation in L_1 is not duplicated in L_2, as in the following,

L_1	L_2		
"M:a"	"T:a"	1/1	2/2
"N:b"	"T:a"	1/1	3/3

the resulting correspondence sets do not differ from those typical of tagmemic merger with regular replacement (cf. 3.2.1.1); thus superficially, both merger (without "syncretism") and split give rise to the same correspondence sets between daughter languages. Needless to say, this presents a dilemma for reconstruction. Fortunately, however, if the data are evaluated in light of certain criteria preliminary to comparative reconstruction, one may ascertain thereby which of the two types of change has occurred, and accordingly reconstruct the correct sequence of events.

Proceeding diachronically from the protolanguage to a daughter language, fundamental differences may be detected between merger and split by differentiation. These characteristics and their consequences will be crucial for setting the criteria which enable us to recognize the occurrence of one type of change over the other in daughter languages. Merger is best viewed as a change that distinguishes a daughter language (or several daughter languages) from the parent language; in a simple case, emic units that are in contrast in the parent language no longer contrast in L_1, but they remain in contrast in L_2. In such a situation comparative reconstruction, which retrieves two-to-one replacements (as well as one-to-one replacements), will correctly reconstruct two emic units in the parent language, as was demonstrated in 3.2. Split by differentiation, on the other hand, is best viewed as a change that distinguishes an early period of a daughter language from a later period of that daughter language; that is, noncontrasting coetic units in an early stage of L_1 are replaced by contrasting emic units in a later stage of L_1. There is no evidence that coetic variants which participate in this process and which differ from the point of view of manifestation mode can be attributed to the parent language as well as to the earlier stage of the daughter language that undergoes such differentiation. In fact, there is evidence that such etic variants should not be attributed to the parent language, as the following data will indicate. Thus, if differentiation is internal to a daughter language, one should not expect that procedures of comparative reconstruction, which retrieve elements in the parent language of two daughter languages, can be employed to detect this linguistic change. However, it will be seen directly that because phonological differentiation is incidental to a special type of merger (so-called secondary split), it may indeed be retrieved via comparative reconstruction, although morphological and syntactic differentiation cannot.

There are ready prototypes to support the above statements about merger and differentiation in phonology, morphology, and syntax. In phonological merger, for example, if we view Middle High German as an early stage of the parent language of Pennsylvania German and Modern Standard German, it is clear that the phonemes /ü/ and /e/ which merge in certain environments in Pennsylvania German (but not in Modern Standard German) to give /e/ were in contrast in Middle High German; cf. MHG *künnen* 'can, be able', MSG *können*, PG *kenne* and MHG *kennen* 'know, recognize', MSG *kennen*, PG *kenne*. (Some details of dialectal vocalic shifting, readily available in handbooks dealing with the diachronic phonology of Modern Standard German, are not essential for this illustration, and have thus been omitted; cf. for example Bach 1961).

In phonological differentiation, on the other hand, complementary coallophones that develop to become contrasting phonemes may be traced back to an earlier stage of a daughter language, but not to the protolanguage (especially from the point of view of manifestation mode). For example, in certain environments the reflex of PIE /t/ becomes /þ/ in early Germanic, via Grimm's Law. Then, as was pointed out by Verner, /þ/ developed a voiceless allophone [þ] in initial position and medially when immediately preceded by a syllable bearing the (mobile) accent characteristic of Proto-Indo-European, and a voiced allophone [ð] when in medial voiced surroundings immediately preceded by an unaccented syllable, as well as in final position. At a later period in Germanic, the mobile accent became fixed upon the root initial syllable; and in cases where the formerly accented and nonaccented syllables were replaced by accented syllables (i.e., merged), the voiceless and voiced phones came to contrast. As has been demonstrated by Hoenigswald (1960:93f.), such phonological differentiation, also known as secondary split, is indeed retrievable by comparative reconstruction. For example, in comparing certain Old Saxon and Sanskrit cognates, such as Old Saxon (OS) *warð* '(I) became', *wurdun* '(we) became' (where OS -*ð* < Gmc. [þ] and OS -*d*-<Gmc. [ð]) and Sanskrit (Skt.) *vavárta* 'I have turned', *vavṛtimá* 'we have turned', respectively (cf. Krahe 1963b:87f. and Prokosch 1939: 60–68), one may observe that Old Saxon voiceless and voiced fricatives resulting from differentiation correspond to a single reflex of the Proto-Indo-European voiceless dental stop in Sanskrit. Because the merged environment (i.e., the accented syllable) containing these fricatives in Old Saxon corresponds to two environments (i.e., accented and unaccented syllables) containing the stop in Sanskrit, whose ancestor did not undergo the particular differentiation that the ancestor of Old Saxon did, one may conclude that differentiation occurred in Germanic, rather than that merger occurred in Indic, and thus correctly reconstruct one protophoneme for Proto-Indo-European, rather than two. Thus comparative reconstruction is applicable in this case only because phonological differentiation arises from secondary split (i.e., it involves a merger of formerly "contrasting" environments).

In morphological merger, if we again view Middle High German as an early stage of the parent language of Pennsylvania German and Modern Standard German, it is clear that the morphemes {first-person-plural-present-indicative}, {second-person-plural-present-indicative}, and {third-person-plural-present-indicative}, which merge in varieties of Pennsylvania German (but not in Modern Standard German) to give {plural-present-indicative}, were in contrast in Middle High German; cf. MHG *nem-en, nem-et, nem-en;* MSG *nehm-en, nehm-t, nehm-en;* PG *nemm-e.*

In morphological differentiation, on the other hand, complementary root coallomorphs that develop to become contrasting morphemes may be traced back to an earlier stage of a daughter language, but not to the parent language (especially from the point of view of manifestation mode). For example, in Early New High German, the verb *wägen* 'to weigh, consider' had two coallomorphs in complementary distribution in the present tense, *weg-* and *wig-*. During the sixteenth century (cf.

Kluge 1963:860), however, there was a redistribution in the environments of these coallomorphs, yielding two verbs that contrast to the present day in content and expression, *wägen* 'to ponder, consider' and *wiegen* '(transitive) to weigh (something)' and '(intransitive) to weigh, be heavy'. In comparing these present-day German verbs with their English cognate, *weigh*, however, one cannot know from a superficial inspection of the resulting correspondence sets whether merger has taken place in English, or whether differentiation has occurred in German. Of course, if Old High German and Old English are available to us, the question may be answered on the spot, since Old High German (and Middle High German) had only one verb, *wegan*, and so did Old English (and Middle English), namely *wegan*. If, however, such early stages of these languages are not available, an observation put forth by Hoenigswald (1960:68) serves as a specific criterion which enables us to detect differentiation in German:

> Doublets contrasting by members of morphophonemes *(honor: honos)* reflect the superaddition of analogic change over the effects of sound change; *so do, in a less clear fashion, differentiated paradigms* [italics mine—JC].

One need think only of verbs like *befehlen, empfehlen, gebären, lesen, sehen,* and *stehlen,* whose "irregularities" in the present tense are also the result of (phonological) secondary split.

In another example of morphological differentiation, root coallomorphs that are in sporadic alternation (i.e., free variation) develop to become contrasting morphemes that can be traced back to an earlier stage of a daughter language, but not to the protolanguage (especially from the point of view of manifestation mode). According to Hockett (1958:273), the English verbs *hoist* and *heist* constitute such a case of differentiation. Diachronically, the events took place as follows: "... the speakers of a language [are] neatly divided, by some geographical line of demarcation, into two groups: those on one side of the line pronounce a certain word in one way, while those on the other side pronounce it in another way.... Now so long as the difference is correlated with dialects, we do not speak of sporadic alternation. But situations of this kind are not stable. Some people, in due time, hear... [both pronunciations]... and sooner or later some speakers acquire both habits of pronunciation, using now the one and now the other in a quite random and unpredictable way. When this has happened, we have sporadic alternation." Later on, pairs like "... *hoist* and *heist* are not two shapes of a single morpheme, but different morphemes, with similar but distinguishable meanings." In comparing these English verbs with their Dutch cognate, *hijsen*[1] 'to raise something with a rope or a (light) block and tackle', however, one cannot determine from a superficial inspection of the resulting correspondence sets whether merger has taken place in Dutch or whether differentiation has taken place in English. Again, if Middle English and Middle Dutch are available to us, the problem may be resolved immediately, since fifteenth-century English had only one verb, *hysse* (cf. the *New English Dictionary on Historical Principles,* or *Oxford English Dictionary* [OED], p. 1316), and so did Middle Dutch, namely *hischen* (Kluge 1963:311). If such early stages of these languages were not available, however, the following observation put forth by Hoenigswald (1960:68) would serve as a criterion which retrieves the split in English:

> Doublets contrasting . . . [other than by members of morphophonemes] reflect dialect borrowing.

Cf. the dialect variants *hoity-toity* and *highty-tighty* (OED p. 1317); older *hoik* and *hike* (replaced by *yoikes*) (OED p. 3862); *boil* (dermatological) and *bile* (OED p. 242); ME *boye* and *baye, bye* (OED p. 260); and *oil* and *ile* (OED p. 1982).

In another example of morphological differentiation, inflectional coallomorphs that are in free variation develop to become contrasting morphemes that may be traced back to an earlier stage of a daughter language, but not to the protolanguage (especially from the point of view of manifestation mode). Consider the Lithuanian case endings for the accusative, the allative, the illative, the locative, and the adessive. According to Senn (1966:92ff.), the allative, illative, and adessive are secondary cases: the allative is the reflex of an old postpositional phrase which contained a noun in the genitive singular or plural, followed by the postposition *p(i);* the illative is the reflex of an old postpositional phrase which contained a noun in the accusative singular or plural, followed by the postposition *na;* and the adessive is the reflex of an old postpositional phrase which contained a noun in the locative singular or plural (or occasionally in the dative or accusative singular), followed by the postposition *p(i).* In preliterary Lithuanian, direction was expressed via the accusative as well as via postpositional (and prepositional) phrases; likewise, location was expressed by means of the locative as well as via postpositional (and prepositional) phrases.

---

1. In all likelihood, the ancestor of this Modern Dutch word was borrowed into an earlier stage of English (and into a good number of other European languages as well; cf. the references in Kluge 1963 and the *New English Dictionary on Historical Principles* [OED]). Interestingly enough, although the borrowing in itself is incidental to the case of differentiation under discussion, it lends further support to the notion that the coallomorphs involved in differentiation cannot be traced back to the parent language, which in this instance would be Proto–West Germanic.

Even before the sixteenth century, however, the postpositions used in the postpositional phrases had become encliticized to the extent that they, together with the archaic endings to which they had become fused, could be considered new case endings, the allative and illative in free variation with the accusative, and the adessive in free variation with the locative. By the sixteenth century, however, the allative, illative, and adessive had developed their own specialized content, though their origin was still transparent. In comparing all of these Lithuanian cases (which have survived, albeit in less transparent form, until the present) with those of Sanskrit, however, one cannot determine from a superficial inspection of the resulting correspondence sets whether merger has taken place in Sanskrit, or whether differentiation has taken place in Lithuanian. Again, if the oldest Sanskrit and the oldest Lithuanian are available to us, the problem could be resolved easily, since Sanskrit has only accusative and locative forms, and in Old Lithuanian, the allative, illative, and adessive forms are more easily recognized as former postpositions suffixed to primary case endings, than they may be today, as was mentioned. If such early stages of these languages were not available to us, however, the following would serve as criteria to retrieve the split in Lithuanian:

(a) In a differentiated pair of emic units in L_1, one of the members of the pair corresponds neatly, with respect to its manifesting mark, to an emic unit in some sister language; the other member of the pair will not so correspond, and its parametric distribution will be narrower than that of the first member (cf. Heller and Macris 1967).
(b) In differentiation with regular replacement (which is equivalent to differentiation with innovation) as well as with semantic change, it may be possible to determine which of these is the source of the manifesting mark of the new emic unit in L_1 by inspection of etic units in a sister language unaffected by differentiation.
(c) In differentiation with borrowing, the source of the manifesting mark may be determined by inspection of the language in which the mark originated.

The Lithuanian endings for the accusative *(vilk-a* 'wolf') and locative *(nami-ē* [*<-ei*] 'at home') correspond to those of the Sanskrit accusative *(vṛk-am* 'wolf') and locative *(vṛk-e* [*<-oi*] 'wolf'), respectively, whereas the Lithuanian allative *(Jōn-o-p* 'to John'), illative *(Jōn-a-n* 'to John') and adessive *(Diev-ie-p* 'with God') have no correspondences in the Sanskrit noun declension; moreover, their parametric distribution is quite limited as opposed to that of the accusative and the locative (cf. Senn 1966:92–95; 434–40). We must look to regular replacement (i.e., innovation) as the source of the new manifesting marks in this instance, since semantic change and borrowing cannot be verified as sources.

On the basis of phonological and morphological comparative reconstruction, Indo-Europeanists have reconstructed an optative and subjunctive conjugation for Proto-Indo-European, and have assigned to them the discourse-level functions of wish and volition, respectively. Accordingly, the tagmemes "Wish:OptSent" and "Volition:SubjSent", which merge in Italic (but not in Hellenic) to give "Volition: . . ." in Italic, were in contrast in Proto-Indo-European. The consequence of these phonological and morphological comparative reconstructions, namely, that a merger has taken place in Italic, is supported furthermore by Italic and Hellenic evidence that goes contrary to the foregoing criteria. It is not the case that only one of the members of the pair "Wish: . . ." and "Volition: . . ." in Greek corresponds neatly, with respect to its constituents, to "Volition: . . ." in Italic; on the contrary, Italic "Volition: . . ." has fillers which correspond in Hellenic either to "Wish: . . ." or to "Volition: . . .". Moreover, in Hellenic, the parametric distribution of "Wish: . . ." is for all practical purposes equal to that of "Volition: . . ." (cf. 2.2.2.1).

In tagmemic differentiation, on the other hand, the freely varying coallotagmas that develop to become contrasting tagmemes may be traced back to an earlier stage of a daughter language, but not to the parent language (especially from the point of view of manifestation mode). For example, in Early New English, the discourse-level Response tagmeme had two freely varying coallotagmas, 'Response: *(do*-less) DeclarSent' and 'Response:*(do)* DeclarSent'. During the eighteenth century, there was a redistribution in the environments of these coallotagmas yielding two tagmemes that contrast to the present day in content and expression, "Response:DeclarSent" and "Affirm: AffSent" (cf. 2.3.1.1). In comparing these English tagmemes with their corresponding tagmeme in German, "Response:DeclarSent", however, one cannot know from a superficial inspection of the resulting correspondence sets whether merger has taken place in German or whether differentiation has taken place in English. Again, if Old High German and Old English are available to us, the question may be answered on the spot, since Old High German had only "Response:DeclarSent", and so did Old English. But if such early stages of these languages are not available, then these criteria will serve to retrieve the differentiation in English. In the English pair "Response:DeclarSent" and "Affirm: AffSent", only the first tagmeme corresponds neatly, with respect to its filler, to the German tagmeme "Response:DeclarSent"; the second does not.[2] Moreover, the

---

2. The construction found in colloquial European German (and in Pennsylvania German [cf. Buffington and Barba 1965:135f.] and Yiddish [cf. Birnbaum 1979:272] as well), *er tut Karten spielen,* is not functionally (i.e., tagmemically) equivalent to English *he does play cards,* since it indicates not an affirmation, but a response with iterative aspect.

parametric distribution of the second is narrower than that of the first. (To attempt an exposition of parameters of discourse to demonstrate this latter point goes beyond the scope of this section; nevertheless, most readers will agree, I believe, that in English the number of contrastive discourse-level environments for "Affirm: . . ." is smaller than the number for "Response: . . .").

All of the preceding remarks concerning tagmemic merger and tagmemic differentiation apply also, mutatis mutandis, to syntagmemic merger, involving, for example, "OptCl [. . .]" and "SubjCl [. . .]" in Hellenic and "SubjCl [. . .]" in Italic (cf. 2.2.2.2), and to syntagmemic differentiation, involving, for example, "V [. . .]" and AffV [. . .]" in English, and "V [. . .]" in German (cf. 2.3.1.2).

To return to the correspondence sets in the first paragraph of this section (3.3.1.1), if one applies the criteria on page 56 to these sets, and determines thereby that they are a product of differentiation in L_1 rather than merger in L_2, then one may represent the sequence of linguistic changes graphically as figures 35, 36, and 37.

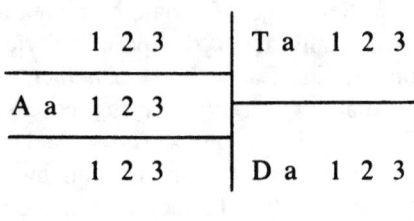

Fig. 35

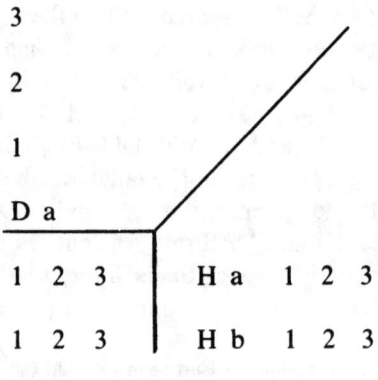

Fig. 36

Allosyntagmatic Reconstruction

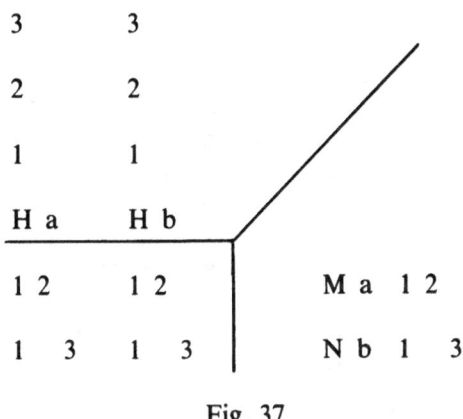

Fig. 37

For an example, see the discussion of the Modern English Response and Affirmation tagmemes on page 57. (In this replacement pattern subtype, and in all the following, if there is duplicate split, the change is irretrievable, and the case appears to be equivalent to emic one-to-one replacement, almost certainly with some etic noncorrespondence.)

3.3.1.2. Syntagmemic. If the split by differentiation occurs only in L_1, as in the following,

L_1	L_2			
"M[a]"	"T[a]"	1/1	2/2	
"N[b]"	"T[a]"	1/1		3/3

the correspondence sets are identical to those typical of syntagmemic merger with regular replacement (cf. 3.2.1.2). As in the preceding similar case of tagmemic differentiation (3.3.1.1), however, the criteria proposed on page 56 may enable us to determine that the above syntagmemic correspondence sets are a result of differentiation in L_1 rather than a merger in L_2. If so, it is possible to describe the sequence of events graphically as figures 35, 36, and 37. For example, we may detect differentiation when we note that the Modern English syntagmemes "V [. . . +VH:v]" and "AffV [+AffAux:affaux +VH:v]" correspond to the Modern German syntagmeme "V [. . . +VH:v]" as described on page 57.

60 Syntactic Change and Syntactic Reconstruction

3.3.1.3. Allotagmatic. If the split is limited to L_1, as in the following,

L_1	L_2		
'M:a/b'	'T:a'	1/1	2/2

the correspondence set is not distinguishable from that typical of allotagmatic merger with regular replacement (cf. 3.2.1.3). The following criteria, however, which are similar to those on page 56, may be used to distinguish etic split from etic merger:

(a) When split results in a pair of coetic units belonging to one emic unit in L_1, only one of the members of the pair corresponds neatly to an etic unit belonging to a corresponding emic unit in some sister language; the new member of the pair will not so correspond.

(b) In etic split with regular replacement (which is equivalent to etic split with innovation), as well as with semantic change, the source of the new etic unit may be determined by inspection of etic units in a sister language unaffected by etic split.

(c) In etic split with borrowing, the source of the new etic unit may be determined by inspection of the language in which the etic unit originated.

Thus it may be possible to determine that the foregoing allotagmatic correspondence set is a product of split in L_1 rather than of merger in L_2, and if so, we may trace the sequence of linguistic events in allotagmatic split graphically as figures 38 and 39.

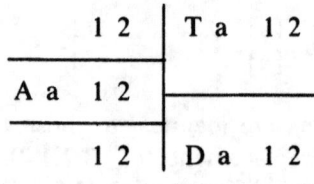

Fig. 38

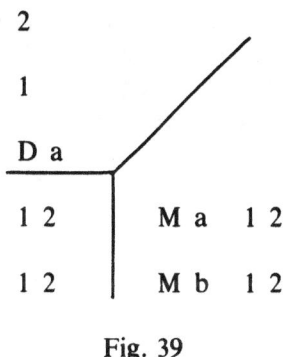

Fig. 39

3.3.1.4. Allosyntagmatic. If there is split in L_1, but not in L_2, as in the following,

L_1	L_2		
'M[a/b]'	'T[a]'	1/1	2/2

the resulting correspondence set is equivalent to that typical of allosyntagmatic merger with regular replacement (cf. 3.2.1.4). As in 3.3.1.3, however, if the criteria on page 60 lead one to conclude that the foregoing allosyntagmatic correspondence set is a result of split in L_1 rather than of merger in L_2, one may then illustrate the sequence of events in allosyntagmatic split graphically as figures 38 and 39.

3.3.2. Replacement with Semantic Change

3.3.2.1. Tagmemic. The term *differentiation with semantic change* may apply to each of the two contrasting replacements of a prototagmeme. For example, in the following correspondence set (which is superficially the same as the set of correspondences in 3.3.1.1),

L_1	L_2			
''M:a''	''T:a''	1/1	2/2	
''N:b''	''T:a''	1/1		3/3

the replacement of 'A:a' by 'M:a' may technically be viewed as semantic change if the distribution of 'M:a', 1 and 2, does not match that of its ancestor protoallotagma 'A:a', 1, 2, and 3; moreover, if in this illustration the filler of ''N:b'' belonged to a prototagmeme other than ''A:a'', say ''B:b'' in 1 and 4, then the presence of the filler of

"B:b" in L_1 in 1 and 3 also constitutes semantic change. If the differentiation occurs in L_1 only, though the resulting correspondence sets are identical to those typical of tagmemic merger with semantic change (cf. 3.2.2.1 and 3.2.1.1), the first criteria (p. 56) may enable us to determine that the foregoing correspondence sets are a result of differentiation in L_1 rather than merger in L_2. If this is the case, it is possible to describe the sequence of events graphically as figures 40, 41, and 42.

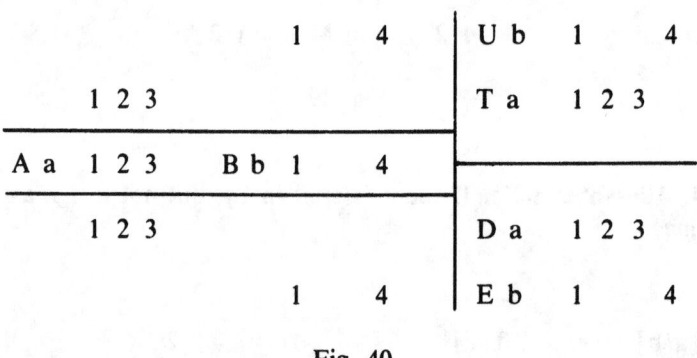

Fig. 40

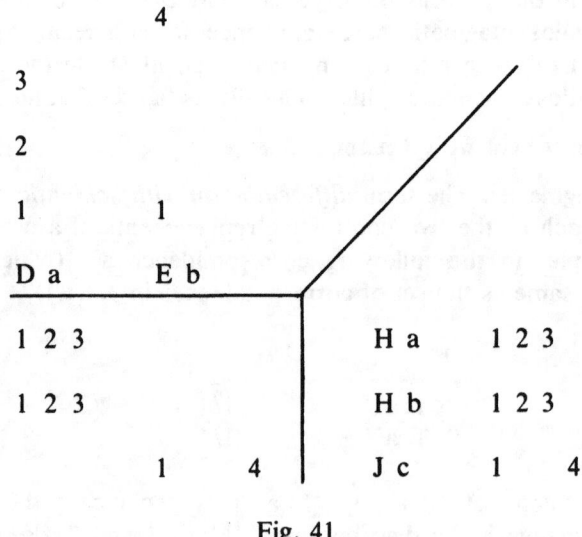

Fig. 41

Allosyntagmatic Reconstruction

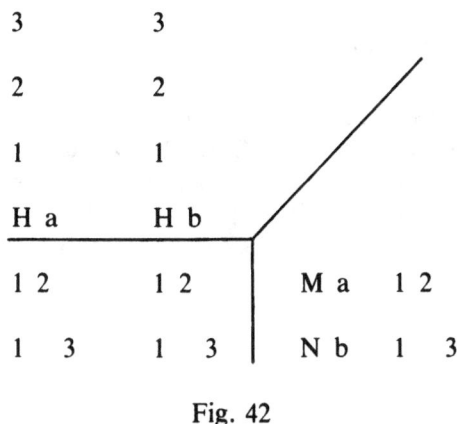

Fig. 42

3.3.2.2. Syntagmemic. As with the prototagmeme in 3.3.2.1, the term *differentiation with semantic change* may apply to each of the two contrasting replacements of a protosyntagmeme. For example, in the following correspondence set (which is superficially identical to the set of correspondences in 3.3.1.2),

L_1	L_2			
"M[a]"	"T(a)"	1/1	2/2	
"N[b]"	"T[a]"	1/1		3/3

the replacement of 'A[a]' by 'M[a]' may technically be viewed as semantic change, if the distribution of 'M[a]', 1 and 2, does not match that of its ancestor protoallosyntagma, 'A[a]', 1, 2, and 3; moreover, if in this illustration the allosyntagma of "N[b]" belonged to a protosyntagmeme other than "A[a]", say "B[b]" in 1 and 4, then the presence of the allosyntagma of "B[b]" in L_1 in 1 and 3 also constitutes semantic change. When the differentiation in L_1 is not duplicated in L_2, the resulting correspondence sets do not differ from those typical of syntagmemic merger with semantic change (cf. 3.2.2.2 and 3.2.1.2). If one applies the criteria on page 56 to the foregoing correspondence sets and determines thereby that they are a product of differentiation in L_1 rather than merger in L_2, then one may represent the sequence of linguistic changes graphically as figures 40 followed by 41 and 42.

3.3.2.3. Allotagmatic. If there is split in L_1 but not in L_2, as in the following,

L_1	L_2		
'M:a/b'	'T:a'	1/1	2/2

the resulting correspondence set is equivalent to that typical of *regular* (cf. 3.2.1.3) but not *semantic* (cf. 3.2.2.3) allotagmatic merger. If the criteria on page 60 lead one to conclude that the foregoing allotagmatic correspondence set is a result of split in L_1 rather than of merger in L_2, one may then illustrate the sequence of events in semantic allotagmatic split graphically as figures 38 and 43.

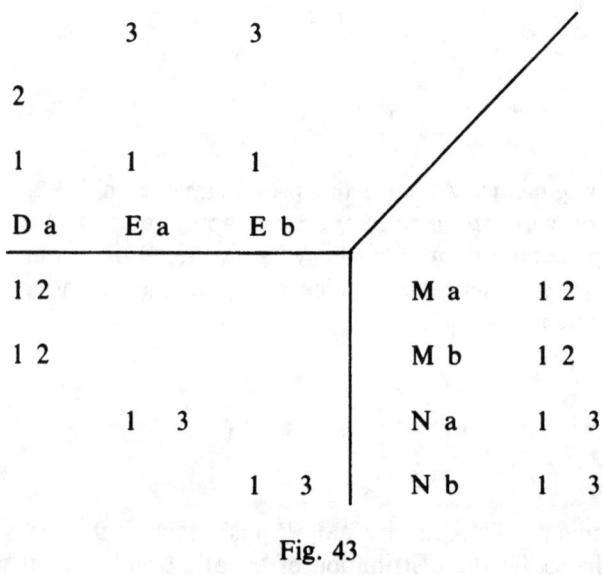

Fig. 43

3.3.2.4. Allosyntagmatic. If the split is limited to L_1, as in the following,

L_1	L_2		
'M[a/b]'	'T[a]'	1/1	2/2

the correspondence set is not distinguishable from that typical of *semantic* (cf. 3.2.2.4) allosyntagmatic merger, but not from that of

Allosyntagmatic Reconstruction

regular (cf. 3.2.1.4) allosyntagmatic merger. Considering the criteria on page 60, however, if it is possible to determine that the foregoing allosyntagmatic correspondence set is a product of differentiation in L_1, rather than of merger in L_2, we may then trace the sequence of linguistic events in semantic allosyntagmatic split graphically as figures 38 and 43.

3.3.3. Replacement with Borrowing

3.3.3.1. Tagmemic. If the differentiation with borrowing occurs only in L_1, as in the following,

L_1	L_2		
"M:a"	"T:a"	1/1	2/2
"N:b"	"T:a"	1/1	3/3

(where the source of the filler of "N:b" is borrowing), the correspondence sets are identical to those typical of regular tagmemic merger (cf. 3.2.1.1). If the criteria proposed on page 58 enable us to determine that the foregoing correspondence sets are a result of differentiation in L_1, rather than merger in L_2, it is possible to describe the sequence of events graphically as figures 35, 36, and 37, where the source of 'H:b' is innovation.

3.3.3.2. Syntagmemic. If the differentiation with borrowing in L_1 is not duplicated in L_2, as in the following,

L_1	L_2		
"M[a]"	"T[a]"	1/1	2/2
"N[b]"	"T[a]"	1/1	3/3

(where the source of the filler of "N[b]" is borrowing), the resulting correspondence sets do not differ from those typical of regular syntactic merger (cf. 3.2.1.2). If one applies the criteria on page 56 to the foregoing correspondence sets and determines thereby that they are a product of differentiation in L_1 rather than merger in L_2, then one may represent the sequence of linguistic changes graphically as figures 35, 36, and 37, where the source of 'H[b]' is borrowing.

3.3.3.3. Allotagmatic. If there is split with borrowing in L_1, but not in L_2, as in the following,

L_1	L_2		
'M:a/b'	'T:a'	1/1	2/2

(where the source of 'M:b' is borrowing), the resulting correspondence set is equivalent to that typical of regular (cf. 3.2.1.3) allotagmatic merger. If the criteria on page 60 lead one to conclude that the foregoing allotagmatic correspondence set is a result of split in L_1 rather than of merger in L_2, one may illustrate the sequence of events in allotagmatic split with borrowing graphically as figures 38 and 39. For example, we may detect split when we note that the Southeastern Pennsylvania German passive allotagmas 'PasAux:pasaux [+auxnuc: auxst]' and 'PasAux:pasaux [+auxnuc:auxst +Conj:conj]' correspond to 'PasAux:pasaux [+auxnuc:auxst]' in other varieties of Pennsylvania German (cf. 2.3.3.3).

3.3.3.4. Allosyntagmatic. If the split with borrowing is limited to L_1, as in the following,

L_1	L_2		
'M[a/b]'	'T[a]'	1/1	2/2

(where the source of 'M[b]' is borrowing), the correspondence set is not distinguishable from that typical of regular (cf. 3.2.1.4) allosyntagmatic merger. Considering the criteria on page 60, if it is possible to determine that the foregoing allosyntagmatic correspondence set is a product of split in L_1 rather than a merger in L_2, we may then trace the sequence of linguistic events in allosyntagmatic split with borrowing graphically as figures 38 and 39. For example, we may detect split when we note that the Southeastern Pennsylvania German passive allosyntagmas 'PasV [+FinAux:finaux +PasAux:pasaux +VH:v]' and 'PasV [+PasAux:pasaux +VH:V]' correspond to 'PasV [+FinAux:finaux +PasAux:pasaux +VH:v]' in other varieties of Pennsylvania German (cf. 2.3.3.4).

3.4 Amorphous Loss or Disappearance

If the amorphous loss, or merger with $\emptyset$, in L_2 is not duplicated in L_1, as in the following,

L_1	L_2		
"M:a"	$\emptyset$	1/1	2/2

the *inability* to satisfy the following criteria suggests that there has been a merger with $\emptyset$ in L_2, rather than a split of $\emptyset$ in L_1.

(a) For at least one manifesting mark of the emic unit in L_1 there is a cognate manifesting mark belonging to some emic unit in L_2.
(b) The distribution of the emic unit in L_1 is narrower than that of other similar emic units in L_1.

A conceivable situation in which such a correspondence set might arise would be a comparison of Italian (as L_2), which has no interrogative tagmeme—though Latin did—and Russian (as L_1), which does. Cf. 2.4.1 and 2.4.2. If the merger is duplicate, then it is completely undetectable from the data.

3.5 Amorphous Gain or Increment

If the amorphous gain or split of ∅ in L_1 is not duplicated in L_2, as in the following,

L_1	L_2		
"M:a"	∅	1/1	2/2

the ability to satisfy the criteria in 3.4.1 suggests that there has been a split of ∅ in L_1, rather than a merger with ∅ in L_2. A conceivable situation in which such a correspondence set might arise would be a comparison of Gothic (as L_1), which has modal auxiliaries, and Greek (as L_2), which does not; cf. 2.5.1 and 2.5.2. If the split is duplicate, this is irretrievable, and by appearances the case becomes equivalent to emic regular one-to-one replacement.

4 Syntactosemantic Reconstruction

4.1 Tagmemic

So far, I have dealt almost exclusively with only two cells of the four-cell tagmeme, those which Pike and Pike (1982:33) call slot (indicating syntactic function) and class. In this chapter I will briefly discuss the third cell, role (indicating syntactosemantic function), and its use in two possible approaches to syntactosemantic reconstruction.[1] The first approach has its starting point in the "syntactic tagmeme" (i.e., the correlation of a syntactic function slot and a manifesting class), for which the contrastive and characteristic environments are syntactic; the second involves the "semantic tagmeme" (i.e., the correlation of a syntactosemantic role and a manifesting class), for which the contrastive and characteristic environments are syntactosemantic. This nomenclature is not intended in any way to introduce a departure from the four-cell tagmeme; rather it is meant merely to emphasize which of two possible distribution mode approaches may be used to indicate contrastive and characteristic environments. As in previous sections, I shall not deal with the fourth cell, cohesion, since it is not relevant to this discussion.

4.1.1. The Syntactic Tagmeme. In order to carry out syntactosemantic reconstruction using the syntactic tagmeme as a starting point, it is necessary to recognize that in addition to horizontal and vertical allotagmas of a tagmeme (cf. 1.3), there are syntactosemantic allotagmas as well. For example, the syntactic tagmeme "S:N /Pn/Cl . . ." has, among its coallotagmas, the following: horizontally, 'S:N' and 'S:Pn'; vertically, 'S:N [+Det:det +NH:n]' and 'S:N [+NH:n]'; and syntactosemantically, (or, in an alternative notation, 'S::Actor:N' and

---

[1]. In this section I wish only to demonstrate that, in principle, syntactosemantic reconstruction is as practicable as syntactic reconstruction. A full treatment of syntactosemantic reconstruction, along with replacement patterns, goes beyond the scope of the present volume; it is my intention to return to this topic at a future date.

S	N
Actor	-

and

S	N
Undergoer	-

'S::Undergoer:N'). If, after correspondence sets are established between L_1 and L_2, it can be determined that both have the syntactosemantic allotagmas just listed, then according to the second principle of 1.4 (p. 11), we may assign these allotagmas to the protolanguage also.

4.1.2. The Semantic Tagmeme. Just as the role cell provides syntactosemantic coallotagmas for the syntactic tagmeme, the slot cell (along with the horizontal and vertical variants) provides syntactic coallotagmas for the "semantic tagmeme"; e.g., 'O::Undergoer:N' and 'S::Undergoer:N' along with 'O::Undergoer:Pn', 'O::Undergoer:N [+Det:det +NH:n]', and 'O::undergoer:N [+NH:n]', etc., are all coallotagmas of "O/S::Undergoer:N/Pn . . .". In order to carry out syntactosemantic reconstruction via semantic tagmemes, one must first establish correspondence sets of these tagmemes between L_1 and L_2. If one of the environments of the contrastive set, 1, is #__#, and one of the environments of the characteristic environment set, 2, of ". . . ::Undergoer: . . ." is TrCl [+ . . . ::Actor: . . . + . . . ::Statement: . . . __ . . .], and if the semantic tagmeme in question occurs in L_1 and L_2, then according to the first principle in 1.4, that semantic tagmeme may be reconstructed for the protolanguage.

4.2 Syntagmemic

Both the syntactic tagmeme and the semantic tagmeme may be used to reconstruct semantic syntagmemes.

4.2.1. The Syntactic Tagmeme. The filler of a syntactic tagmeme on one level is expanded as a syntagmeme on the next level below; thus, a syntagmeme may be considered to be a vertical allotagma of a tagmeme. Moreover, a syntagmeme, as an expansion of the filler of a tagmeme, may be correlated with the role as well as the slot of that tagmeme, just as the filler is. If, after correspondence sets are established between L_1 and L_2, it can be determined that both share one or more syntactosemantic-vertical allotagmas (which are also syntactosemantic syntagmemes) of a tagmeme, then according to both principles in 1.4, each of these may be reconstructed for the protolanguage.

Consider, for example, two occurrences of the (clause-level) syntactic tagmeme "PAdv:RR" in Modern English:
(1) He jumped *into the water.*
(2) He stayed *in the water.*

In these sentences, the filler, RR, is expanded as the syntagmeme "RR [+Relr:prep +Reld:N]" on the phrase level immediately below the clause level; thus this syntagmeme is a vertical allotagma of "PAdv:RR". In sentences (1) and (2) above, this syntagmeme is correlated with the slot "PAdv: ..."; in (1), however, the syntagmeme is also correlated with the role *goal*, whereas in (2), it is correlated with the role *location*. Thus, syntactically, the syntagmemes under discussion in (1) and (2) do not contrast; rather they are vertical syntactosemantic coallotagmas of "PAdv:RR" (which is in turn a constituent of a syntagmeme on a higher level: "Cl [+S: ... +P: ... +PAdv: ...]"). Now if English as L_1 and say German as L_2 both have the vertical syntactosemantic allotagmas 'PAdv::Goal:RR [+Relr:prep +Reld:N]' and 'PAdv::Location:RR [+Relr:prep +Reld:N]', then according to the two principles in 1.4, we may reconstruct not only the syntactic tagmeme "PAdv:RR", but also each of these vertical syntactosemantic allotagmas (i.e., syntactosemantic syntagmemes) for Proto-Germanic.

4.2.2. The Semantic Tagmeme. Just as in the case of the syntactic tagmeme, so also in the case of the semantic tagmeme, the filler of a tagmeme on one level is expanded as a syntagmeme on the next level below. Thus, this (semantic) syntagmeme is a vertical allotagma of a semantic tagmeme and is correlated with the role (as well as the slot) of that tagmeme, just as the filler is. If, after correspondence sets are established between L_1 and L_2, it can be determined that both share certain semantic tagmemes and their vertical allotagmas (i.e., [semantic] syntagmemes), then according to the principles in 1.4, each of these may be reconstructed for the protolanguage.

Consider, for example, the (clause-level) semantic tagmemes "PAdv::Goal:RR" and "PAdv::Location:RR" in Modern English in the foregoing sentences (1) and (2), respectively. In these sentences, the filler RR is expanded as the syntagmeme "RR [+Relr:prep +Reld:N]" on the phrase level immediately below the clause level; thus this syntagmeme is a vertical allotagma of "PAdv::Goal:RR" in (1) and a vertical allotagma of "PAdv::Location:RR" in (2). If one of the environments of the contrastive set, 1, is #__#, one of the environments of the characteristic set, 2, of "PAdv::Goal:RR" is "Cl [+ ... ::Actor: ... + ... ::Statement: ... __ + ... ::Location: ...]", and one of the environments of the characteristic set, 3, of "PAdv::Location:RR" is "Cl [+ ... ::Actor: ... + ... ::Statement: ... + ... ::Goal: ... __]", then the semantic tagmemes and syntagmemes under discussion in sentences (1) and (2) contrast semantically. If English as L_1 and German as L_2 both share these semantic tagmemes and their vertical allotagmas—i.e., (semantic) syntagmemes—then according to the two principles in 1.4 (pp. 10–11) each of these may be reconstructed for Proto-Germanic.

Bibliography

Algeo, John. 1974. "Tagmemics: A Brief Overview." In *Advances in Tagmemics,* edited by Ruth M. Brend, pp. 1–9. Amsterdam: North-Holland Publishing Company.

Arnauld, Antoine and Claude Lancelot. 1660. *General and Rational Grammar: The Port-Royal Grammar.* Edited and translated (1975) by Jacques Rieux and Bernard E. Rollin. Janua Linguarum, Series Minor, no. 208. The Hague: Mouton.

Bach, Adolf. 1961. *Geschichte der deutschen Sprache.* 7th ed. Heidelberg: Quelle und Meyer.

Birnbaum, Henrik. 1977. *Linguistic Reconstruction: Its Potentials and Limitations in New Perspective.* Journal of Indo-European Studies Monograph no. 2. Washington, D.C.: Institute for the Study of Man.

Birnbaum, Solomon A. 1979. *Yiddish. A Survey and a Grammar.* Toronto and Buffalo: University of Toronto Press.

Bowers, John S. 1981. *The Theory of Grammatical Relations.* Ithaca and London: Cornell University Press.

Brend, Ruth M. 1968. *A Tagmemic Analysis of Mexican Spanish Clauses.* The Hague: Mouton.

Buck, Carl Darling. 1933. *Comparative Grammar of Greek and Latin.* Chicago: The University of Chicago Press.

Buffington, Albert F. and Preston A. Barba. 1965. *A Pennsylvania German Grammar.* Revised edition. Allentown, Penna.: Schlechter's.

Chafe, Wallace. 1959. "Internal Reconstruction in Seneca." *Language* 35:477–95.

Cook, Walter A., S. J. 1969. *Introduction to Tagmemic Analysis.* New York: Holt, Rinehart and Winston.

Costello, John R. 1975. "Vestigial Substantival Adverbs and 'Prepositionalization' in Old Frisian." *Neuphilologische Mitteilungen* 76:651–70.

———. 1977. *A Generative Grammar of Old Frisian*. Bern: Peter Lang Verlag.

———. 1978a. "Rule Simplification and the Reconstruction of Interdialectal Rule Borrowing." *Word* 29:233–40.

———. 1978b. "Syntactic Change and Second Language Acquisition: The Case for Pennsylvania German." *Linguistics* 213:29–50.

———. 1980. "The Absolute Construction in Gothic." In *Studies Presented to Robert A. Fowkes on the Occasion of His Retirement* [*Word*, Vol. 31, No. 1], edited by John R. Costello, pp. 91–104. New York: International Linguistic Association.

Curme, George O. 1931. *A Grammar of the English Language, Vol. 3, Syntax*. Boston: D.C. Heath.

———. 1947. *English Grammar*. New York: Barnes and Noble.

Fillmore, Charles J. 1968. "The Case for Case." In *Universals in Linguistic Theory*, edited by Emmon Bach and Robert T. Harms, pp. 1–88. New York: Holt, Rinehart and Winston.

Friedrich, Paul. 1975. *Proto-Indo-European Syntax: The Order of Meaningful Elements*. Journal of Indo-European Studies, Monograph no. 1. Butte, Montana: Montana College of Mineral Science and Technology.

Gleason, Henry A., Jr. 1961. *An Introduction to Descriptive Linguistics*. Revised ed. New York: Holt, Rinehart and Winston.

Greenberg, Joseph H. 1957. *Essays in Linguistics*. Chicago: University of Chicago Press.

———. 1966. "Some Universals of Grammar with Particular Reference to the Order of Meaningful Elements." In *Universals of Language*, edited by Joseph H. Greenberg. 2nd ed. Pp. 73–113. Cambridge, Mass.: The M.I.T. Press.

Hale, Austin. 1976. "The Relationship of Tagmemic Theory to Rules, Derivation, and Transformational Grammar." In *Tagmemics, Vol. 2, Theoretical Discussion*, edited by Ruth M. Brend and Kenneth L. Pike, pp. 51–89. The Hague: Mouton.

Harris, Zellig S. 1951. *Structural Linguistics*. Chicago: The University of Chicago Press.

Heller, Louis G. and James Macris. 1967. *Parametric Linguistics*. Janua Linguarum, no. 58. The Hague: Mouton.

Heller, Louis G. and James Macris. 1979. "Parameters: Reactance as Analytic Tool and Evidence." *Word* 30:205–13.

Hirt, Hermann. 1934. *Handbuch des Urgermanischen*. Vol. 3. Heidelberg: Carl Winters Universitätsbuchhandlung.

Hockett, Charles F. 1958. *A Course in Modern Linguistics*. Toronto: The Macmillan Company.

Bibliography

Hoenigswald, Henry M. 1960. *Language Change and Linguistic Reconstruction*. Chicago: The University of Chicago Press.

———. 1973. *Studies in Formal Historical Linguistics*. Dordrecht and Boston: Reidel.

Hopper, Vincent F., ed. 1948. *Chaucer's Canterbury Tales*. Great Neck, N.Y.: Barron's.

Jakobson, Roman. 1962. "Typological Studies and Their Contribution to Historical Comparative Linguistics." In *Selected Writings*, pp. 523–32. The Hague: Mouton.

Jespersen, Otto. 1969. *Analytic Syntax*. Reprint (1937). New York: Holt, Rinehart and Winston.

King, Robert D. 1969. *Historical Linguistics and Generative Grammar*. Englewood Cliffs, N.J.: Prentice-Hall.

Kiparsky, Paul. 1971. "Phonological Change." Mimeographed. Bloomington, Indiana: Indiana University Linguistics Club.

Klammer, Thomas P. and Carol J. Compton. 1974. "Some Recent Contributions to Tagmemic Analysis of Discourse." In *Advances in Tagmemics*, edited by Ruth M. Brend, pp. 377–87. Amsterdam: North-Holland Publishing Company.

Kluge, Friedrich. 1963. *Etymologisches Wörterbuch der deutschen Sprache*, edited by Walther Mitzka. 19th ed. Berlin: Walter De Gruyter & Co.

Krahe, Hans. 1963. *Germanische Sprachwissenschaft. Vol. 1. Einleitung und Lautlehre*. 5th ed. Berlin: Walter De Gruyter & Co.

———. 1965. *Germanische Sprachwissenschaft. Vol. 2. Formenlehre*. 5th ed. Berlin: Walter De Gruyter & Co.

Lehmann, Winfred P. 1973. *Historical Linguistics. An Introduction*. 2nd ed. New York: Holt, Rinehart and Winston.

Lewis, Charlton T. 1964. *A Latin Dictionary for Schools*. Reprint (1889). Oxford: At the Clarendon Press.

Lightfoot, David W. 1979. *Principles of Diachronic Syntax*. Cambridge: Cambridge University Press.

———. 1980. "On Reconstructing a Proto-Syntax." *Linguistic Reconstruction and Indo-European Syntax*, edited by Paolo Ramat et al., pp. 27–45. Amsterdam: John Benjamins B.V.

Lockwood, William B. 1968. *Historical German Syntax*. Oxford: At the Clarendon Press.

Longacre, Robert E. 1964. *Grammar Discovery Procedures. A Field Manual*. Janua Linguarum, no. 33. The Hague: Mouton.

———. 1965. "Some Fundamental Insights of Tagmemics." *Language*

41:65–76.

———. 1966. "Trique Clause and Sentence: A Study in Contrast, Variation, and Distribution." *International Journal of American Linguistics* 32:242–52.

———. 1976. Introduction to *Discourse Grammar: Studies in Indigenous Languages of Colombia, Panama, and Ecuador*, Part I, edited by Robert E. Longacre and Frances Woods. Dallas, Texas: Summer Institute of Linguistics and University of Texas at Arlington.

Lyons, John. 1970. *Noam Chomsky*. New York: The Viking Press.

Marchand, James W. 1956. "Internal Reconstruction of Phonemic Split." *Language 32:245–53*.

Melchart, H. Craig. 1981. "'God-Drinking': A Syntactic Transformation in Hittite." *The Journal of Indo-European Studies* 9:245–55.

Muller, Henri F. and Pauline Taylor. 1932. *A Chrestomathy of Vulgar Latin*. Boston: D.C. Heath.

New English Dictionary on Historical Principles. Oxford: Oxford University Press. 1884–1928.

Pike, Kenneth L. 1954. *Language in Relation to a Unified Theory of the Structure of Human Behavior*. Part I. Glendale, California: Summer Institute of Linguistics.

———. 1958. "On Tagmemes nee Gramemes." *International Journal of American Linguistics* 24:273–78.

———. 1959. "Language as Particle, Wave and Field." *The Texas Quarterly* .2:37–54.

———. 1972. "Dimensions of Grammatical Constructions." In *Kenneth L. Pike. Selected Writings,* edited by Ruth M. Brend, pp. 160–86. Janua Linguarum, Series Maior, no. 55. The Hague: Mouton. (Reprinted from *Language 38:221–44*).

——— and Evelyn G. Pike. 1982. *Grammatical Analysis*. 2nd ed. Dallas, Texas: Summer Institute of Linguistics and University of Texas at Arlington.

Prokosch, Eduard. 1939. *A Comparative Germanic Grammar*. Philadelphia: Linguistic Society of America and University of Pennsylvania.

Quirk, Randolph and C. L. Wrenn. 1957. *An Old English Grammar*. New York: Holt, Rinehart and Winston.

Senn, Alfred. 1966. *Handbuch der litauischen Sprache*. Vol. 1. Heidelberg: Carl Winter Universitätsverlag.

Steller, Walther. 1928. *Abriss der altfriesischen Grammatik*. Halle (Saale): Max Niemeyer Verlag.

Streitberg, Wilhelm. 1960. *Die gotische Bibel*. 4th ed. Heidelberg: Carl Winter Universitätsverlag.

Traugott, Elizabeth Closs. 1972. *A History of English Syntax*. New York: Holt, Rinehart and Winston.

Wright, Joseph. 1955. *A Middle High German Primer,* revised by M. O'C. Walshe. 5th ed. Oxford: Clarendon Press.

Index

Allosyntagma, 6–9
Allotagma
    horizontal and vertical, 8–9; 71–73
    syntactic, 1; 4–5; 72
    syntactosemantic, 71–72
Ambiguous environment set (class), 4n
Amorphous gain, 38; 69
    criteria for distinguishing from amorphous loss, 68
Amorphous loss, 37; 68–69
    criteria for distinguishing from amorphous gain, 68
Borrowing, replacement with, 13; 18–19
Bracketing, 6–7
Characteristic environment set (class), 2–4; 6; 14n; 71
Class, 1n; 71–72
Coallosyntagma, 7–9
Coallotagma, 7–9
Cohesion, 1n
Comparative method (see Comparative reconstruction)
Comparative reconstruction
    principles underlying, 9–11
    syntactic, chapter 3 (41–69)
    syntactosemantic, chapter 4 (71–73)
Content, 2–3
Contrast
  among syntagmemes
    syntactic, 6
    syntactosemantic, 72–73
  among tagmemes,
    syntactic, 1–4
    syntactosemantic, 71–72
Contrastive environment set (class), 1–7; 14n; 71
Differentiation, 29
Distribution mode, 1–4; 2n; 5n; 6; 9–11
Emic change, 15n; 15–16
Emic status, 2–7
Emic units, comparative reconstruction of, 9–11; 41–69
Etic change, 15n; 15–16

Etic units, comparative reconstruction of, 9–11; 41–69
Expression, 2–3
Feature mode, 2n
Field, 2n
Filler, 1–2
Function
    syntactic, 1–4; 71–72
    syntactosemantic, 71–72
Grameme, 1–2
Grammatical levels, 5–9
Homonymy, 1–4
Horizontal etic units, 7–9; 71–72
Innovation, replacement with, 13–14
Manifestation mode, 2n; 3; 9–10 15
Merger, 20–29; 47–53
    compared with split, 53–61
    criteria for distinguishing from split, 58; 62
One-to-one replacement pattern, 4–5; 13–20; 41–47
Particle, 2n
Port-Royal Grammar, v; 1
Quotation marks, double and single, 8; 12
Reconstruction diagram, 10
Regular replacement, 13–14
Role, 1n; 71–72
"Semantic change," 14n footnote 1; 16; 24–26; 32–33;
Slot, 1n; 71–73
Split, 29–37; 53–68
    compared with merger, 53–61
    criteria for distinguishing from merger, 58; 62
"Syncretism," 24; 26
Syntactic reconstruction (see Comparative reconstruction)
Syntactosemantic reconstruction (see Comparative reconstruction)
Syntagmeme
  semantic, 72–73
  syntactic, 5–7
    viewed diachronically, 6–7
    viewed synchronically, 5–6
Tagmeme
  as a constituent of a syntagmeme, 5–6
    four-cell, 1n; 71n
  semantic, 71–73
  syntactic, 1; 71–73
    viewed diachronically, 4–5
    viewed synchronically, 1–4
Three-dimensional diagram, 4–5

Index

Transformations, 19–20
    reconstruction of, 42
Tree diagrams, 6–7
Vertical etic units, 7–9; 71–73
Wave, 2n footnote 3
Zero, 37n

www.ingramcontent.com/pod-product-compliance
Lightning Source LLC
Chambersburg PA
CBHW051815230426
43672CB00012B/2745